D0573591

All About
Fertilizers, Soils & Water

Created and
designed by the
editorial staff
of ORTHO Books

Written by
A. Cort Sinnes

Edited by
Shirley Manning

Art direction
and design by
John Williams

Major photography by
Michael Landis

Illustrations by
Ron Hildebrand

T1-BKG-494

Ortho Books

Manager, Ortho Books
Robert L. Iacopi

Editorial Director
Min S. Yee

Editor
Marian E. May

Production Editor
Anne Coolman

Administrative Assistant
Judith C. Pillon

Horticultural Consultant
Michael MacCaskey

Additional
photography by
Michael McKinley
Ann Ashley
Clyde Childress
Colin McRae

Proofreading by
Editcetera
Berkeley, CA

Indexing by
Baxter & Stimson

Typography by
Terry Robinson & Co.
San Francisco, CA

Color Separations by
Color Tech Corp.
Redwood City, CA

Printed by
Webcrafters
Madison, WI

Cover printed by
Graphic Enterprises
of Milwaukee, Inc.
Milwaukee, WI

Photo research by Carousel—Winfrey
Page 52: Webb Photo
Page 61: TVA
Page 63: PFI

Acknowledgement:
Egger & Son, Mill Valley, CA
for loan of plant materials
used in photography

Address all inquiries to:
Ortho Books
Chevron Chemical Company
Consumer Products Division
575 Market Street
San Francisco, CA 94105

Copyright © 1979
Chevron Chemical Company
All rights reserved under
International and Pan-American
Copyright Conventions

No portion of this book may
be reproduced without written
permission from the publisher

We are not responsible
for unsolicited manuscripts,
photographs, or illustrations

1 2 3 4 5 6 7 8 9 10

ISBN 0-917102-80-0

Library of Congress Catalog
Card Number 79-52992

All About Fertilizers, Soils & Water

Good Garden Practices

Good garden practices are the result of lessons
learned from one gardening season to the next.
Just reading a book can't take the place of experience
in the garden, but the information on these pages combined
with your experience should result in a better garden.

This book is dedicated to:
The home gardener who has been confused for years when trying to figure out which fertilizer to apply to what plant . . .

The beginning gardener who tries to discern how much is enough water . . .

The gardener with a clay soil who reads the disturbing advice on the back of a seed packet: "Plant in a rich, well-drained loam as soon as the soil has warmed . . ."

And to gardeners everywhere who expect better than average results from the plants in their gardens.

Soils, water and fertilizers are among the most important determinants of good plant growth. Besides these, other influences include temperature, radiant energy, biological factors, and the combined effects of temperature, light, and length of growing season as they relate to the variety of the plant and other genetic factors.

When you talk about growing plants or about gardening in general, you're talking about all the factors influencing plant growth. While a full discussion of all these factors is impossible in one book, you will find, in these pages, in-

formation important enough to be considered an indispensable tool.

In this book we try to combine over-the-fence neighborly advice with some of the more technical information about soils, water and fertilizers. You don't have to be a scientist to be a good gardener, but understanding the principles

behind certain natural phenomena can help make good gardening a less mysterious process.

If you've gardened for more than a couple of seasons you've probably developed some of your own habits and practices as they concern soil, water and fertilizers. And if you're like most gardeners after a

Left and right: No matter how diverse—in location, style or size—all successful gardens have one thing in common: their owners follow the same basic good garden practices. These practices have been proven from one season to the next, for as long as there have been gardens.

couple of seasons, you begin to discover which methods and products work the best in your own garden, and return to them year after year. The knowledge based on personal experience is particularly valuable in gardening, but it doesn't completely take the place of some "book-learning."

To that end we have combined on these pages information aimed at the beginning as well as the more advanced gardener—information that is difficult to find in other books and manuals. At this point you may not be interested

in all the information contained in this book. Our intent was to provide you with a source of information that can answer questions at various different points in your gardening career.

You may wonder whether all this information is really necessary, especially if the best gardener you know is part of the "guess-or-by-golly" school who doesn't know the difference between one fertilizer and another. There's no denying that there appear to be many of these gardeners around, but on closer inspection, you'll probably find that their success lies in the same principles discussed in this book. A plant can't tell the difference between a novice gardener and a person with a Ph.D. in botany— as long as they both supply what the plant needs for good growth.

The Home Garden

While the selection may be diverse, the total number of plants in an average home garden is comparatively small, and it is usually possible to treat each plant individually. With simple handtools and the products available at local garden centers, home gardeners have a chance to apply the principles of soil and water manage-

ment over a wide range of plant/soil combinations. And the home gardener can apply these principles much more precisely than the farmer can with a few crops in big fields.

While the home gardener has some advantages over the farmer and commercial grower, one big difference should be pointed out: when selecting land for a commercial farm, the quality of the soil is of primary importance to the farmer. The home gardener, on the other hand, considers the house first and accepts whatever land comes with it. Rarely can anyone buy with the house stone-free, "rich loam" soils that appear over and over again in the words of gardening experts. More often than not, the soils around the house are not naturally well-suited to the plants that you want to grow, especially if builders have destroyed the natural surface soil and left a thin topsoil over fill layers of trash and subsoil.

And so it is that many new home gardeners begin with soils

that are too hilly, too sandy, too clayey, too dry, too wet or too infertile for good gardens. But good garden soils can be made from them, and the information found in this book will help in that process.

Bear in mind, though, that not all plants have the same requirements. A garden might include lawns, perennial and annual flowers, vegetables, fruit trees and a variety of ornamental shrubs and trees. Some prefer slightly acid or neutral soil. Others do best in strongly acid ones. Some plants need a very fertile soil; others do fine in poor soil.

For home gardeners, the central

problem of soil management is to develop and maintain a proper relationship between each plant and the soil immediately around it. And it is possible to make several different soils to fit the requirements of different plants, all in the same garden.

Aside from pure luck, a gardener's success depends on knowing

two sets of factors: the requirements of the different plants that can be grown in the particular climate, and the characteristics of the soils (either naturally-occurring or man-made) in the garden. Match the two requirements well, follow some basic good garden practices, and you'll have a successful garden.

In the Yearbook on Soil published in 1957 by the U.S. Department of Agriculture, Charles Kellogg stated:

"One could hardly overemphasize the critical relationship between a plant and the soil in which it grows. Admiration of a plant in the catalog, at a flower show, or in a friend's garden is not enough basis for deciding to put it in our own garden, unless we know that its requirements can be satisfied by our garden soil as it is or as we can change it.

"A large money budget is not necessary for a good garden, even on poor soil. Far more important is the work budget—the care and attention the garden will be given through the seasons . . ."

How to Use This Book

This book is laid out in three main chapters—soil, fertilizers, and water—ending with a section called Special Handling and a glossary of gardening terms.

The subject of soil can be a complex one, and obviously, one of primary interest to all garden-

Even if your garden is measured in inches and the plants are confined to containers, you still need to know the basics of soils, fertilizers and water to achieve the best results.

ers. We have devoted a sizeable part of this book to the discussion of many aspects of soil as it relates to the home gardener—from a short course in soil science to a discussion of rototillers. A few of the areas of interest might be: what you should know about earthworms, page 16; how to take a soil test and read the returned report, pages 20-23; an indepth look at a variety of mulches and soil amendments on pages 30-37; and how to make compost and the bin to make it in, pages 46-47.

The first part of the fertilizer chapter discusses the nutrients found in fertilizers, their effects on plant growth and the differences and similarities between natural organic and synthetic formulations.

If you're trying to decipher the information on a fertilizer label, see pages 60-63. If you want to know more about the ways to apply fertilizers, read pages 68-71. If you can't tell one fertilizer from another, see the spread on pages 64-65. And if you want to know about a particular plant, or group of plants that may need special attention in the soil, water, or fertilizer department, see pages 84-95 for Special Handling instruction.

In the watering chapter we've taken a close look at how soil character influences watering practices, and given some general rules answering the question "how much is enough?" If you've ever wondered whether or not to sprinkle plants lightly during a heat spell, or when is the best time to water, see pages 75-77.

On the following spread, pages 8-9, you'll see a detailed drawing of how a plant grows and an explanation of the basic requirements of plant growth. An understanding of the information on those two pages can greatly help in understanding much of the material in the rest of this book.

Acknowledgements

A book on the combined subjects of fertilizers, soils and water relies heavily on established facts and figures. In this we are indebted to the United States Department of Agriculture and their numerous and informative yearbooks. Fertilizers, soils and water are also the subject of much recent research and investigation. We would like to acknowledge the part played by Richard Hildreth, Director of the State Arboretum at Utah, and Michael Reisenauer at the University of California at Davis for keeping us accurate and up-to-the-minute.

We would also like to acknowledge the Brooklyn Botanic Garden for their research into soils, and their experiments in converting subsoil into topsoil, found on page 44 of this book, and Professor Wesley P. Judkins and Floyd F. Smith for the use of their article on organic gardening found on pages 66-67.

Our debt to the state universities and extension services continues to grow. The information they generously make available provides us with the means to know more about regionalized problems and their solutions. Particularly, we would like to acknowledge the Division of Agricultural Sciences of the University of California, Texas A & M Extension and Research Center, and the Auburn University Extension Service in Alabama.

For his research and writing on organic fertilizers and compost, thank you Sam Wilson. And thanks to George Hawkes and Al Crozier, from within our own organization, for donating generously of their time and advice on the technical aspects of this book.

The Basic Requirements of Plants

A simple fact is this: plants will grow, indeed thrive, if certain basic requirements are met. In the following pages are the ins and outs, the general information and the details, on how to best meet those basic requirements.

These are a plant's basic requirements for growth:
1) Air
2) Water
3) Nutrients
4) Suitable environment, including proper temperature and light, and protection of the plant's leaves and roots.

Air in the soil

When the roots of plants are deprived of air, by any means, you can expect trouble.

In clay soils, the space between soil particles (the pore space) is very small. When water seeps into the soil, it drives out air by filling the pore spaces. The plant in such a situation, if prolonged, declines in vigor and the unwary gardener waters some more, killing the plant with kindness.

There are more ways to deprive roots of air than by filling the pore spaces with water. When a soil crusts over after a hard rain, the air supply to the roots is partially cut off. Soils are often deprived of their full complement of air by compaction of the top layer of the soil. Compact the soil by wearing a footpath across the lawn, and you kill the grass.

Observe a tree in a school ground or park where foot traffic is heavy. If you find the soil is packed down on the surface—compacted—you know that the tree is struggling for survival. The compacted soil makes the water run off instead of moving into the soil, and at the same time chokes off the supply of air to the roots.

A regular and uniform supply of moisture

Neither too much, nor too little. Too much water can cause plant roots to die, especially if drainage through the soil is poor. On the other hand, too little water will result in "water stress," and possibly death.

Water has been called the "hazardous necessity." It is easy to kill a plant with too much water. Plant roots require moisture and air for growth. The roots require a growing medium through which air can move, bringing oxygen to them and removing the carbon dioxide they respire.

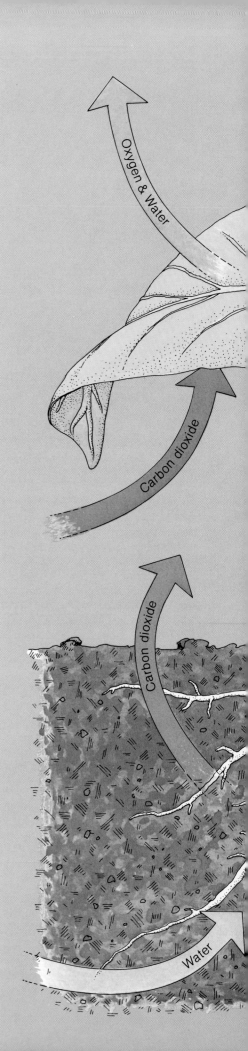

Leaves

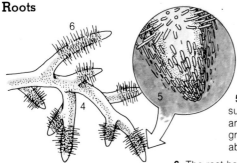

1. Leaves produce food for the plant and release water and oxygen into the atmosphere.

2. Chloroplasts are the chlorophyll bodies within cells in which photosynthesis takes place in order to manufacture carbohydrates (starches and sugars) for the plant. They give the leaf its green color.

3. Stomata are specialized "breathing" pores through which carbon dioxide enters and water and oxygen are released. They close when water is limited or under other stress.

Roots

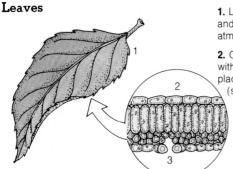

4. Feeder roots grow from the lateral roots and serve to transport water and nutrients absorbed by root hairs. They tend to be concentrated within the "dripline" (where the rain drips off the tree), but some may extend great distances.

5. Root caps produce a continuous supply of new cells that are sloughed off and serve to lubricate the advance of the growing root tip through the soil as it absorbs water and nutrients.

6. The root hairs are microscopic appendages to the feeder roots; root hairs absorb water and nutrients.

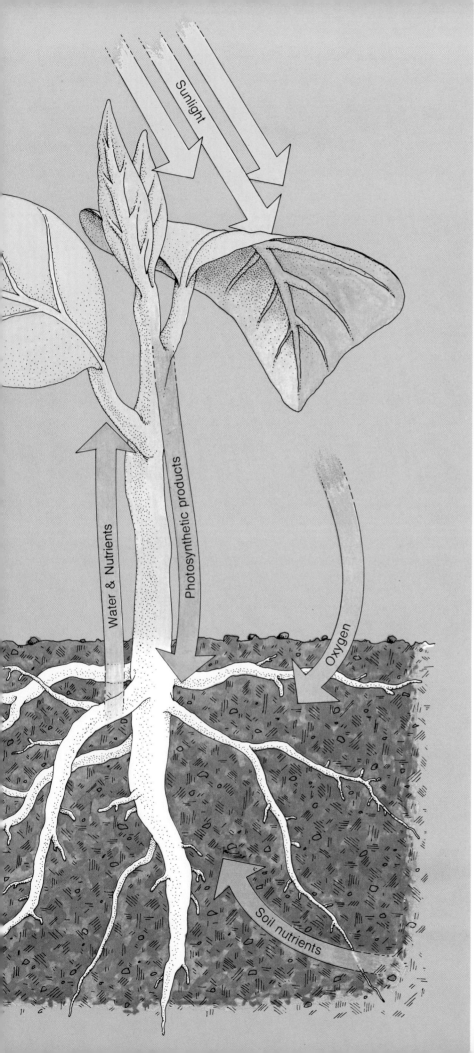

Sunlight

Water & Nutrients

Photosynthetic products

Oxygen

Soil nutrients

Stop the supply of air by filling the air spaces in the soil with water for too long a time, and root growth is retarded. The longer the air is cut off, the greater the damage to the roots, and subsequently to the plant.

What it boils down to is this: roots are all-important in supplying the plant with what it needs to grow, and they are most commonly damaged in two ways: (1) the surface soil becomes compacted, or the structure of the soil itself has too few or too fine pore spaces (such as clayey soils), and water can't move through fast enough, so it kills the roots, or (2) too much water is applied, which causes the pore spaces in the soil to stay saturated with water, and the roots drown.

A continuous and uniform supply of nutrients

The requirements of plants for nutrients is continuous, and the small daily amount needed should always be available. With some slow-growing plants, the daily needs are very small and you can wait until the condition of the plant tells you its nutrient needs are not being met—the yellowing leaf tells you that nitrogen may be deficient. But waiting for a plant to give you a sign that it needs nutrients is not the best garden practice for most plants, especially for vegetables. With these fast-growing, short-season plants there should be enough fertilizer in the soil to see them through from start to finish. Any check in growth due to lack of nutrients will reduce yields and perhaps the quality of the vegetable.

In applying fertilizers—liquid or dry, simple or multinutrient, fish or blood meal, or manure—follow label directions. Don't try to outguess the manufacturer by adding more than the recommended amount. Too much of anything, including manure, is dangerous.

Protection of leaves and roots

Leaves and roots need protection from temperature extremes, strong winds, birds and beasts, weed competition, and pests and diseases. But if your plant has the right amounts of air, moisture and nutrients, the plant should be healthy and more resistant to these potential threats.

Soil

There are many kinds of garden soils, from sand, to loam, to clay. You can find a plant to grow in any soil, or change the soil to grow any plant—the choice is up to you.

Soil is a word that means different things to different people. The engineer, the farmer and the home gardener all have a special relationship with soil, but the type of information each needs may be quite different.

The information in this chapter is intended for the home gardener who, most often, thinks of soil as the substance plants grow in. Because few of us are naturally blessed with the "rich, well-drained garden loam" referred to so often on the back of seed packets, our relationship with soil usually begins in earnest when we have to do something to improve what we have.

Don't try to live with an unfavorable soil—nothing can dampen the enthusiasm of a gardener more quickly than soil that is hard to manage. It may even be true that the mythical green thumb is closely related to a good knowledge of soil.

It should be noted, though, that some plant can be found for almost any kind of soil. The results would be a garden dictated not by the gardener's desires, but by the natural limitations of that gardener's soil. On the other hand, almost any kind of soil can be

Long-time gardeners know their plot of ground—the characteristics of the soil, how much to water, when to get the soil ready for planting, and what fertilizer to use. Some of the most valuable gardening knowledge is based on experience.

modified to grow any plant that's right for the climate if the gardener is willing to go to the trouble. Most successful gardeners try to find satisfying combinations of plants that require a minimum of soil change for good growth. And for all but the worst soils, changing the soil so that it supports a wider variety of plants is not a particularly extensive or complicated process. Any good gardener will tell you that it's worth the trouble.

Made rich with the yearly addition of a variety of organic matter, soil can be the gardener's prized possession. Instead of needing a rototiller, soil of this quality is worked easily with only a shovel.

What is Soil?

Before we set about changing soil, we need to know what soil is.

Traditionally, soil's relationship to the earth is compared with the rind's relationship to an orange. The analogy is apt if you imagine an orange with a rind that is highly irregular in width, color, texture and composition. Be it deep or shallow, red or black, sand or clay, the soil is the link between the rock shell of the

Early Soil Science

The first classification of soils is believed to have taken place in China approximately 4,200 years ago. This classification was based on the soil's ability to produce certain crops and was used to determine "property" taxes.

As far as recorded history goes, we don't know much else about agriculture and soil science until Roman times. The Romans had several good manuals for farmers, prepared by keen observers who sifted out the best from the experience they saw around them. Columella's *Husbandry*, written about 60 A.D., was a handbook for fifteen generations.

After Rome fell, the people of Europe were disorganized and lived in a dark age of disease, famine and war for more than a thousand years. The actual knowledge behind European agriculture during the long period to the French Revolution and for some time afterward was the knowledge of the farm people themselves, passed on by father and mother to son and daughter. Their practices were highly traditional and slow to change. Yields of crops were low, and disasters frequent.

But Arabian culture flourished in the Near East, North Africa and southern Spain. Crop yields there were reasonably good, especially under irrigation. In the 12th century, for example, Ibn-al-Awan, a Moorish scholar, prepared an excellent handbook on agriculture. The experience he recorded and explained became significant to us much later through the early Spanish settlements in the southwestern United States.

In the 16th century, Bernard Palissy maintained that manures and plant residues returned to the soil the "salt" that plants removed. He regarded the ash left when plants burned as "a kind of salt" and the "principle" of plant growth. But experimental results were disappointing before chemistry had developed the skills necessary to distinguish among the many kinds of "salt."

Jan Baptista van Helmont, a Flemish chemist, thought he had proved water to be the "principle" in a famous experiment with a willow tree in about 1635. He planted a small tree in 200 pounds of oven-dried soil. After growing 5 years, protected from dust and given only rainwater, the tree was removed. The soil was redried and weighed. Because the soil loss was only 2 ounces (which could be considered experimental error) and the tree had gained 165 pounds, van Helmont assumed that growth was due to the water alone. Now we know that the 2 ounces were critically important nutrients and that the bulk of the 165 pounds was carbon, oxygen and hydrogen, taken mostly from the air and water. His results were widely accepted, however.

The French scientist, Antoine Lavoisier, who was led to the guillotine in 1794, contributed great skills. Building on earlier work, as every scientist does, he perfected the quantitative balance with which tiny amounts of substances can be weighed. He also developed a table of chemical elements. It was incomplete, but it was a remarkable forward step. He showed that plants and animals used oxygen and survived by respiration—the "burning" of organic food. He and others thus were able to explain the heaviness of Van Helmont's willow tree.

But the great change in agricultural theory came in 1840 when a German chemist, Justus von Liebig, published his findings. He made careful analyses of surface soils and plants, and stated the balance sheet of plant nutrition: "The crops on a field diminish or increase in exact proportion to the diminution or increase of the mineral substances conveyed to it in manure."

Most farms in western Europe were small and intensively cultivated, but America was a big place with lots of room. Within a few years after clearing, the native fertility of the relatively acid and nutrient-poor soils along the Atlantic seaboard was exhausted. Many agriculturists emphasized the need for lime, fertilizers and rotations with clover. But for more than a hundred years after the American Revolution, it was comparatively easy for young people to move further west to soils that were richer and had not been previously farmed.

Although homesteading ended about 1910, the U.S. public and many farmers and professional agriculturists did not see the serious problems of soil management that were coming. Farming during the early years of this century generally was exploitative, and most systems of soil management were planned on a short-run basis despite the warnings of Ruffin, Hilgard, Hopkins, and King—some of the far-sighted American soil scientists of the time.

After the First World War, agriculture was depressed. It was hard to adjust total production downward from the great increases stimulated by the war. Along with the continuing soil depletion, the shrinking market meant that farmers could scarcely make ends meet.

The land grant colleges were well established and were becoming better, but they had to cover all phases of agriculture in their teaching programs. Consequently, the efforts devoted to soil science were small in relation to the growing soil problems on farms.

In the 1920s the Department of Agriculture, and H. H. Bennett in particular, started writing dramatically about the growing soil problem, which became worse just when the general depression deepened.

Bennett and his staff developed a grouping of the many kinds of soil under the "use-capability" concept. They classified soils and related the different types to how each should be used and improved. This started the conservation program on a sound basis. It pointed out the major conditions each land user must deal with and furnished a guide to the combinations of practices required for sustained production.

Adapted from "We Seek; We Learn" by Charles Kellogg, The Yearbook of Agriculture 1957, U.S.D.A.

earth and the living things on its surface. We are dependent on soils for life itself.

Geologists are primarily concerned with the earth's crust—a shell of solid rock about 20 to 30 miles thick surrounding the earth. Soil scientists, on the other hand, are concerned with the thin layer of loose material that covers this shell. This layer, the soil, can be anywhere from a few inches to a few feet thick.

Every solid rock, when it is exposed at the surface of the earth, slowly disintegrates into loose material through the process called weathering. Rocks are broken up into smaller particles by frost action, by the expansion and contraction caused by temperature changes, by the grinding action of streams, glaciers and wind, and by the force of large tree roots. This physical weathering is aided by chemical weathering processes, which cause the rock minerals to dissolve slowly and change by the action of water, carbon dioxide, oxygen, organic acids, and the effects of microbial activity.

So here is this rather thin layer of loose material—mineral elements from weathered rocks, dead and living organic matter (both flora and fauna), air and water—lying on top of a thick layer of solid rock and constantly undergoing change from the effects of weather, chemical processes, microbes, plants and man. This, then, is soil. Or is it?

When, in fact, does the loose material become soil? There is no definite answer, but it is usually called soil if it is supporting plant life. There is no minimum or maximum thickness necessary for material to be called soil. What is required is that the material be a medium in which plant roots can grow and from which they can obtain water, air and the nutrient elements essential to plant growth.

What is soil composed of?

Soils, by their very nature, are constantly undergoing change. Every soil consists of mineral and organic matter, water, air and living organisms. The proportions may vary but the major components remain the same.

Ignoring air and water temporarily, we can say simply that soil is made up of different sizes of particles of two general types: mineral and organic. They are often referred to as the "mineral fraction" and the "organic fraction." The particles are of weathered and unweathered mineral grains from the original rocks, new minerals that have formed in the soil, living microorganisms and organic matter in all stages of decay.

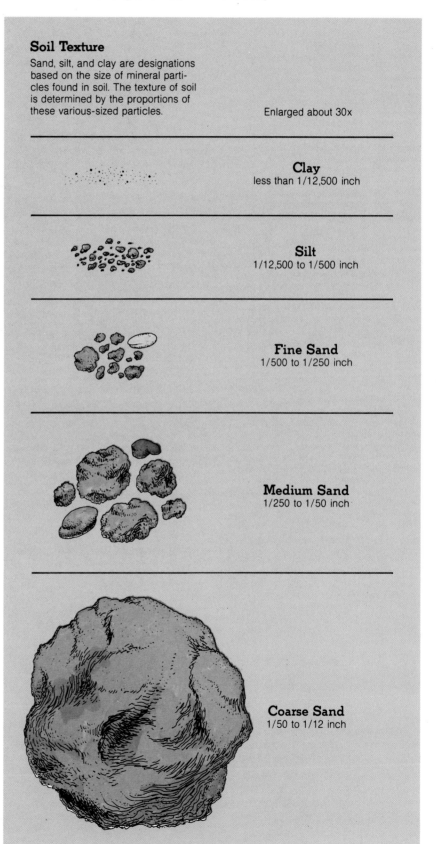

Soil Texture
Sand, silt, and clay are designations based on the size of mineral particles found in soil. The texture of soil is determined by the proportions of these various-sized particles.

Enlarged about 30x

Clay
less than 1/12,500 inch

Silt
1/12,500 to 1/500 inch

Fine Sand
1/500 to 1/250 inch

Medium Sand
1/250 to 1/50 inch

Coarse Sand
1/50 to 1/12 inch

Many things can be determined by the "feel" of the soil. A handful of soil that falls apart after being squeezed is dry enough to be spaded or tilled easily.

The Mineral Fraction

Scientists have defined three basic sizes of particles to describe the mineral portion of the soil mixture. These are called (in order of decreasing size) sand, silt and clay. All soils are mixtures, in one proportion or another, of these types of particles.

There's a simple test to estimate the proportion of each particle type in any particular soil. Moisten the soil and rub some of it between your thumb and fingers to determine its "feel."

The sands are harsh and gritty, and the particles scarcely hold together at all. Loamy sands are gritty, too, but the particles cling together when moist. At the other extreme, clay can be squeezed into a smooth smear. A silt loam makes a rough and broken smear. A clay loam smear is not as smooth as a clay's, nor as broken as a silt loam's. Loams give only a very rough smear; sandy loams give scarcely any.

In addition to influencing the feel or texture of the soil, each of the particle sizes contributes somewhat different properties to the soil as far as a plant is concerned. The properties affected by particle size are: water percolation, water retention, aeration, nutrient supply, nutrient release rate, nutrient storage, buffering or resistance to chemical changes, and the resistance to change in temperatures.

The mineral fraction also provides a plant with most of the essential nutrients it needs for growth.

The Organic Fraction

Organic matter is a broad term which includes living soil microorganisms, plant roots, manure, compost, dead and decomposing animals, insects, leaves, stems, sawdust and many other substances. Whether it is living or in any of the various stages of decomposition, organic matter is what makes up the organic fraction of the soil. It is safe to say that any soil in its natural state contains some organic matter, but the proportions from soil to soil vary widely. And let it be known from the start that no matter what type of soil you have, organic matter is an important friend of the gardener, one that has a leading role in any soil improvement program.

Organic matter is the food of the microorganisms that inhabit the soil in incredible numbers. A thimbleful of soil may contain as many as two billion bacteria, about thirty million fragments of fungi and perhaps a hundred thousand protozoa. Most of these microorganisms are beneficial, indeed vital, to plants. Here's why:

At any one time organic matter can be called a substance, but looked at over a period of time, it is more accurately seen as a dynamic process—the effects of countless microorganisms keep organic matter in an almost constant state of change. These microorganisms use organic matter for food—as a source of energy. They use the nutrients in the organic matter for a while, and then pass them on in a form usable by plants. Soil organic matter usually contains 5 to 6 percent nitrogen, nearly all of which *cannot* be used by plants until the microorganisms have converted it to a form of "available" nitrogen.

Newly added organic matter undergoes various process changes which last anywhere from a few months to a number of years, and ends in a more or less stable product called humus. We'll talk more of humus later, but we emphasize here that, because the microorganisms need food to fuel their activities, it is important to add fresh organic matter back to the garden soil at least once a year.

Organic matter influences not only the fertility of the soil, but also its structure. When organic matter is added to the soil, it has a number of beneficial effects during the process of decomposition.

At opposite ends of the scale, the most difficult soils are clays and those with a sandy texture. Clay soils may retain too much moisture and are difficult to manage. Sandy soils do not retain enough moisture, and because water moves so rapidly through them, nutrients are quickly leached out. Organic matter mixed into a clay soil improves its drainage and allows air to move more readily through the soil, warming it up earlier in the spring. Organic matter incorporated into sandy soils will hold moisture and nutrients in the root zone. The more organic matter you incorporate into a sandy soil, the more you increase its moisture-holding capacity. The addition of organic matter makes any soil easier to work, giving it a soft and loamy consistency—what the old-timers refer to as a *mellow* soil.

Clay

Mention the word clay to a gardener and you usually get a shudder; it may be great for bricks and pottery but as a planting medium, unimproved clay is one of the most difficult soils to work with. Although clay is considered as part of the mineral fraction of soil, it has some special qualities and a bad reputation that deserve separate consideration here.

The clay particles are the smallest particles of the mineral fraction.

Because of their extremely small size they have a tendency to pack and become dense, shutting out both air and water. But take a look at the soil triangle on page 17 and note that clay can also be part of the best garden soils. At their best, the clay particles are aggregated.

This involves the grouping of the individual soil particles into larger secondary units, called aggregates or granules. Many factors play a part in aggregation.

Excessive amounts of clay can lead to very bad soil structure, but in proper amounts clay can act as a conditioner, binding soil particles into granules.

The binding of various particles of soil together into granules is one of the characteristics of the best garden soils. Clay particles provide the main nutrient reservoir against loss by leaching, holding the nutrients for later use by the plant. So clay is not always the bad guy it is made out to be: in proper proportions, clay can have a positive effect on soil structure, fertility and water retention.

Your Own Soil

To learn more about your own garden soil you must dig, not simply on the surface but down to about 3 feet—even more if you suspect deep hardpans or other barriers to roots and water. The lower layers of soil control the supplies of nutrients and water to the deep roots, and have an important role in water drainage.

Most soils consist of a series of definite layers, called horizons, one above the other, with different colors and other properties. The horizons have been produced by the longtime effects of the climate and vegetation acting on the mineral matter. The horizons collectively are called the soil profile. Very "young" or mechanically mixed soils may not have horizons. Examples include soils in the flood plains along streams, recent sand dunes and soil made by earthfills. If you dig into an ordinary upland soil and find no regular horizons, you can be reasonably certain that the soil has been moved about and mixed up not long ago.

Some of the most important things to look for when digging in your garden soil are depth, structure, color and texture.

Depth
The dark colored topsoil is normally the most mellow and the most fertile. The topsoils of the greatest depth are the black soils developed under grass, such as those in Iowa and the Dakotas. In contrast, the topsoil is normally very thin in the desert—and on steep slopes—and only moderately thick under the forests of humid regions. Builders of new homes often destroy the layer of

topsoil completely or may cover it over with raw, earthy material from other excavations.

Under the topsoil is the layer called the subsoil, and it is here that the problems of a soil may originate. This material may be loose and porous to great depths, or there may be no subsoil over hard rocks, with the topsoil providing very little space for roots and water storage. Such soils generally can support only drought-resistant plants that normally have shallow roots. For more about shallow soils, see Problem Soils, page 38.

Structure
In the ideal garden soil, the individual soil particles are grouped together into fairly stable crumbs or granules. These crumblike aggregates provide the best soil structure. The next best structure is a soil with slightly larger, blocky, nutlike aggregates. The worst soils of all are the structureless soils.

There are two extremes of structureless soils: sands and clays. In

sandy soils, each grain is a particle by itself with no substance to bind one particle to another. Such soils hold little water between rains and are easily blown about by the wind.

Clays, on the other hand, can be massive soils (think of a dense, heavy mass) with no regular structural forms. Clayey soils become even worse if plowed, driven on or walked on when they are wet. Clayey soils can exist as topsoils or beneath topsoils as a layer or layers of hardpan. Wherever it occurs within the depth of normal rooting for garden plants, such a massive soil must be reworked to make it granular or blocky. It is not enough simply to break up massive clods of clay. Organic matter must be added, or else the clay particles will flow back together into masses when they are wet again.

Color
Soil color by itself is not important, but it indicates other conditions that are. Along with other evidence, color can tell the garden-

How does your soil rate in "good drainage"?
The ideal soil is one that holds moisture and at the same time allows a constant flow of air through the soil—bringing oxygen to the roots and removing carbon dioxide from the soil. The ideal soil is a combination of the good points of sand and of clay. Sand provides fast drainage and good aeration, but fails in the water-holding department. Clay is tops in water-holding ability, but dangerously low in supplying air to the soil.

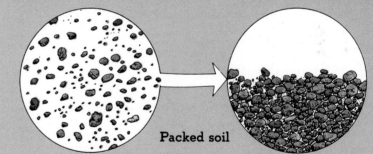

Packed soil

Individual, non-aggregated particles pack into a solid mass with no space for air or water.

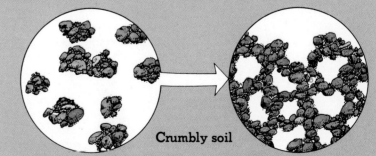

Crumbly soil

Cultivation and the addition of organic matter aggregate the particles into porous crumbs or granules.

When water fills all the spaces in the soil, air is forced out and plants may drown. In well drained soil there is a film of water and air in each space.

er a great deal about drainage, the amount of organic matter in the soil and its general level of productivity.

Brownish black and dark brown generally suggest a good supply of humus. Black surface soils in low ground suggest muck and poor drainage, but some black soils—such as many in the Midwest that have developed under tall grass—are well drained.

Red or yellow soils generally (again, not always) suggest fairly good drainage. Yellow suggests leaching and a low supply of plant nutrients, as do the grays or whites in upland areas of good drainage. White colors in dry regions may indicate that the soils are too salty for most plants.

Texture and soil types

A brief recap of what we know so far: Soil is made up of mineral particles of different sizes and shapes, organic matter in various stages of decomposition, and air and water. The predominant size of the mineral particles and the amount of organic matter are what determine the character of the soil. The size and quantity of both the organic and the mineral particles also determine the amounts of air and water that are in the soil at any one time. But the textural class a soil belongs to is determined by the size and proportions of the mineral fraction alone. Finding out which class of soil you have in your garden is not difficult and can provide helpful information.

We've already noted that the basic classification of soils depends on the size of the mineral particles: sand, silt and clay— from largest to smallest. A soil that is 100 percent sand, silt or clay is rare, so to properly describe soil texture, scientists have named the various classes as: loamy sand, sandy loam, silty loam, loam, sandy clay loam, clay loam, silty clay loam, sandy clay and silty clay. These classes are all determined by the percentages of sand, silt and clay they contain. The soil textural triangle on page 17 can be used to classify a particular soil.

Garden soils of the intermediate textures—the sandy loams, loams and silt loams—are the easiest to handle and make the best garden soils. In these soils the characteristic properties of sand, silt and clay are in the right proportions to balance their effects on water retention and percolation, aeration, and nutrient supply. Because of these intermediate properties, loam soils are capable of growing a wide variety of crops. (For more about loams, see What is Good Soil?, page 18.)

A simple experiment with fairly accurate results can be performed to determine the textural class of your soil. The steps in the experiment are explained in the illustration below. Carry out this same test using soil from different places in your garden. Then chart each of them by marking off the layers on a piece of paper held up to the jar as shown in the illustration. If the particles divide into about 40 percent sand, 40 percent silt and 20 percent clay, you can call your soil loam—a good soil to have. If your soil falls into another classification, you may want to add organic matter to change it (see Problem Soils, page 38).

Earthworms

When conditions are favorable, earthworms are the dominant animal life in the soil—at such times, their weight equals or exceeds that of all the other soil-dwelling animals combined. Earthworms number several million to an acre in favorable soils, and their total weight per acre may be as high as one-half ton.

Earthworms flourish in well-drained soils that contain abundant organic matter and a continuous supply of available calcium. They are susceptible to drought, cold, waterlogging, and extremes of acidity or alkalinity.

Earthworms are important agents in mixing surface organic residues with the underlying soil. The earthworms in an acre can bring to the surface 20 tons of soil a year. Their burrowing activity is most intense in the top 6 inches, although some tunnels extend to depths of 6 feet. Earthworm channeling improves soil aeration and increases movement of water into and through soils.

Earthworms contribute to the formation of soil structure by their cast-forming activities. In feeding, the earthworm ingests soil and organic wastes. The residue, combined with the calcium carbonate and mucus secreted from the gut wall, is ejected as a granular cast.

Few people disagree that, if present in large enough numbers, earthworms can help improve soil structure. But there are sharp differences of opinion concerning the relationship of earthworms to soil fertility. Some persons insist that earthworms almost single-handedly are responsible for good soil fertility. Because the organic residues ejected by earthworms are poorer in nutrients than the original residues ingested, such a viewpoint has little basis in fact. And there is no good evidence that passage of soil particles through a worm's gut increases the availability of the nutrients they contain.

What can be said is this: The beneficial effects of earthworms on plant growth are largely those associated with improved aeration and improved tilth. In the final analysis, earthworms should be considered an indication of a good soil fertility rather than its cause.

Determining soil texture

Fill a quart jar about ⅔ full of water. Add soil until the jar is almost full. Screw on the jar top and shake it vigorously. Then let the soil settle. In a short time the heaviest sand particles sink to the bottom and the sand layer becomes visible, but the silt and clay particles will take hours to settle out. The very fine clay particles are so small that the molecular action of water itself will keep them in suspension indefinitely.

Carry out this same test using soil from different places in your garden. Then chart each of them by marking off the layers on a piece of paper held up to the jar. Compare your results with the charts at right.

Note: To achieve the best stratification, use about 1 teaspoon of a dispersing agent per quart of water. Or add a little Calgon, which contains such an agent.

Soil textural classes

The percentages of sand, silt and clay determine the texture of any soil.

The upper chart indicates—very approximately—the percentages of sand, silt and clay in the major soil textural classifications. There is a wide range in the percentages for any given soil class. You can compare these proportions with your own soils' texture if you carry out the experiment described on the opposite page.

The lower chart is the traditional triangle used to classify specific soils. The soil classifications do not change abruptly—one gradually eases into the next. If your soil is about 15% clay, 65% sand and 20% silt, it would be classified as "sandy loam"—it is in that area of the triangle that the three percentage lines intersects.

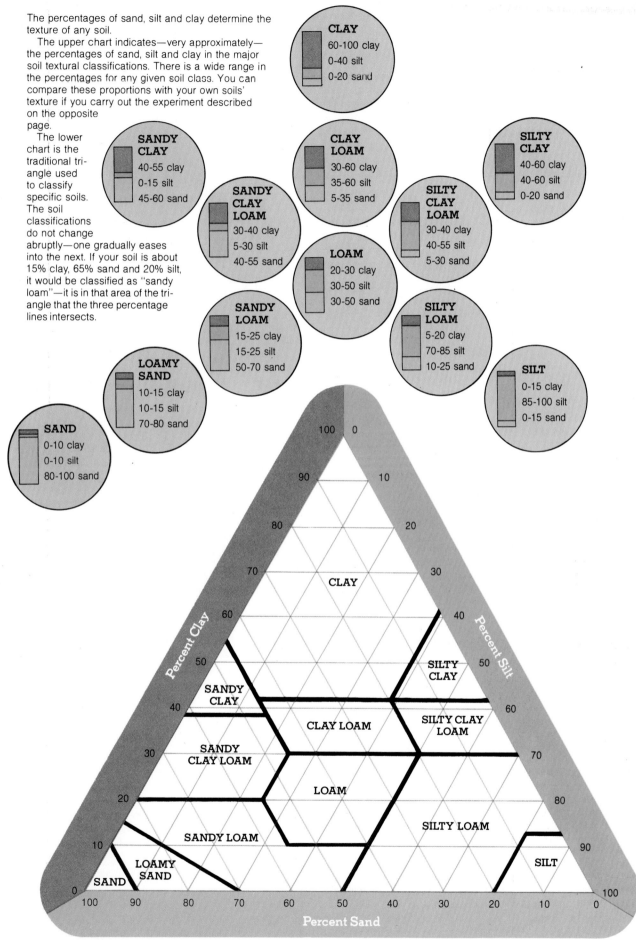

CLAY
60-100 clay
0-40 silt
0-20 sand

SANDY CLAY
40-55 clay
0-15 silt
45-60 sand

CLAY LOAM
30-60 clay
35-60 silt
5-35 sand

SILTY CLAY
40-60 clay
40-60 silt
0-20 sand

SANDY CLAY LOAM
30-40 clay
5-30 silt
40-55 sand

SILTY CLAY LOAM
30-40 clay
40-55 silt
5-30 sand

LOAM
20-30 clay
30-50 silt
30-50 sand

SANDY LOAM
15-25 clay
15-25 silt
50-70 sand

SILTY LOAM
5-20 clay
70-85 silt
10-25 sand

LOAMY SAND
10-15 clay
10-15 silt
70-80 sand

SILT
0-15 clay
85-100 silt
0-15 sand

SAND
0-10 clay
0-10 silt
80-100 sand

What is Good Soil?

It's easy to talk at great length about soil in general without ever defining the specific qualities of a "good" soil. In fact, the properties of problem soils are probably better known than the properties of good soils, because unfortunately, more people have poor soils than good ones.

But if you look at soil improvement as an ongoing, long-term program, it's a good idea to know what the ultimate goal is, so that each step is a step in the right direction. Obviously, there are different optimums of soils for different groups of plants, but it's surprising how many plants are content to grow in a range of soils with the same basic qualities: a "good" soil.

Qualities of a good soil are closely related to the functions of soil in general: (1) Soil serves as anchorage for the plant: the roots must be able to penetrate far enough into the soil to anchor the plant securely. (2) The structure of the soil must be such that the roots can readily develop, assuring the plant its full quota of water and minerals. The structure of the soil is related to water percolation and retention characteristics—whether water can move into the soil and whether the soil holds too much, too little or just the right amount—so structure is doubly important. (3) The fertility of the soil: the nutrients necessary for plant growth that are not naturally available in the soil must be added in their proper amounts.

In short, some main points to consider are depth of the soil, its structure and its fertility.

The influential soil scientist, E.W. Hilgard, put it succinctly when he stated in 1906: "The physical condition of the soil must be determined before judging its fertility." To elaborate: a soil may have a plentiful supply of mineral nutrients but still restrict plant growth because of its physical condition. As is shown in the photograph above, the physical condition of the soil must be such that it allows germinating seeds to easily break through the surface layer. Also, the soil must not impede root growth; the easier you make it

on the roots, the better the plant will grow.

In short, the characteristics of a good garden soil would be as follows:
• it is crumbly, and can be easily penetrated by plant roots.
• the individual particles are well aggregated; that is, they are combined into pea-sized or smaller crumbs which are not easily destroyed by rain or irrigation water.

A well-aggregated soil will not crust and prevent seed germination. It's easily worked, and allows rapid water infiltration. And finally, more as a characteristic than a requirement, a good soil supports a thriving population of beneficial soil microorganisms.

So how can you tell if your soil is a "good" one or not? The **depth** of the topsoil can be checked easily enough by simply digging a hole: If you encounter an impenetrable layer (hardpan) in the first two or three feet, the topsoil may not be deep enough to support all the plants you want to grow (see page 39).

A soil test is the best way to determine soil **fertility,** and is strongly recommended. If you choose not to have a soil test performed, any of the general purpose "complete" fertilizers will ensure an adequate supply of essential nutrients, but you may be applying more than you need of some nutrients and less of others.

Soil structure is another story. Some soil tests will indicate the texture of the soil sample, but while soil texture and structure are related, they are not the same thing. **Texture** is formally defined as the proportions of sand, silt and clay particles that make up any soil. **Structure,** on the other hand, refers to the way those particles are held together.

In good soil, the individual particles of sand, silt and clay are in such proportions that they mask the bad qualities in each other without interfering with the good qualities. The various ratios or proportions of sand, silt and clay are many but, as we've already noted, good soils are generally referred to as loams.

Good soils not only have optimum proportions of sand, silt and clay particles, but the particles are held together in aggre-

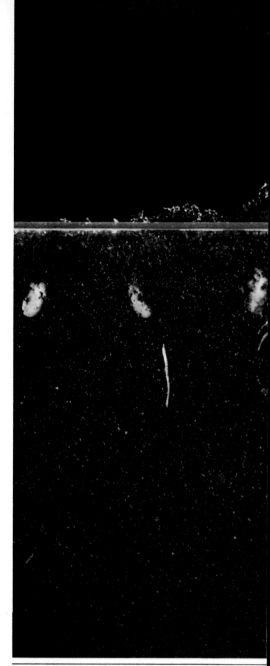

gates that take on properties of their own, distinct from the individual particle's characteristics. In a good soil there is sufficient air space between the aggregates to provide the proper balance between good drainage and water retention, and to allow plant roots space to grow. It is in these spaces or pores between the aggregates that plant roots perform the all-important function of absorbing what the plant needs for good growth: water, nutrients and air in the soil. If these air spaces are too few or too small, the plant can either "drown" from too much water or "suffocate" from lack of air. In extremely sandy soils, where each particle is its own "aggregate," there is plenty of aeration, but water and nutrients are not

retained since the soil can't hold them. (For help in visualizing aggregates, see the illustration on page 15.)

Take a look at the illustration on page 17. You can see that there is quite a range in the proportions that make up different types of loam soil. If you are fortunate, your native soil falls into one of those categories. But if it doesn't, can you ever expect to have a loam soil? The answer is an unqualified yes—there are natural loams and "made loams."

In the case of made loams, the word loam does not refer to the quantity of sand, silt and clay particles, but rather to the working quality of the soil, which is similar, if not identical, to a natural loam.

Getting and Keeping Good Soil

Any discussion of the characteristics of good soil ultimately gets into the subject of organic matter, because *the addition of organic matter is probably the single most important method of improving soils.* Soil particles are held together in aggregates mainly by a by-product of soil microorganisms that use organic matter as their food.

Adding organic matter to your soil as an amendment or conditioner that you incorporate into the soil—or as a mulch that you spread over the top of the soil—is what the gardener can do to help keep the structure of a good soil good. Nature also steps in to

A seed planted in the open ground has a big job to perform. If the soil surface crusts over, the emerging seed may not be able to break through; if the structure of the soil is too dense, the first tender roots may have difficulty in growing.

give you a hand: soil microorganisms break down the organic matter, binding the soil particles together in the process, and the further effects of the sun and wind help particles stick together into aggregates, as do alternate freezing and thawing temperatures in winter.

But when it comes time to plant, the unsuspecting gardener sometimes destroys the structure by *over-cultivating* the soil. Too many passes with a high-speed rototiller can disturb soil structure to the point where aggregation is destroyed (see page 45).

Soil Tests

If you are planning to put in a lawn, vegetable garden, perennial border, flower garden, orchard—any type of garden at all—or if you are having soil-related problems in an established garden, a soil test can solve many mysteries. Taking a test sample and having it analyzed are not lengthy or difficult processes. We feel that it is time well spent: the information contained in the report enables the gardener to be more accurate in improving the soil for specific plants. And making specific, needed improvements is far superior to the hit-and-miss method of adding fertilizers, lime or soil conditioners in unknown amounts.

Who does it?

Some state universities will test soil free of charge; others perform routine tests for a nominal fee. In the few states where universities do not provide this service, you should contact a private soil-testing laboratory: look in the yellow pages of your telephone directory under "Laboratories—Testing." If you do not find a listing, call your county agriculture extension agent and ask for a recommendation. (Note: If you use a private laboratory, inquire first regarding the cost of specific tests.) Home test kits are also available from scientific supply houses and mail order catalogs. Professionals debate the accuracy of such kits, and most feel that if an inexpensive testing service is available, it should be used instead of a home test.

When to test

For unimproved land you should collect samples 3 or 4 months before you intend to plant. This will give you ample time to get the test report back from the laboratory and make the necessary soil improvements before planting. In established plantings, this lead time is not necessary.

Soils should not be sampled when they are wet, since it is difficult to mix the samples properly. A good rule to follow is: If the soil is too wet to plow or cultivate, it is too wet for sampling.

What do you need?

Because most soil labs are set up like an assembly line, they usually provide the customer with a written form, a pint carton for the sample, and a shipping carton. If these are not part of the program in your state, be sure to contact the laboratory before submitting any samples for instructions on how they want them sent in.

The only tools you'll need are: a garden trowel or a shovel and tablespoon, or a soil sampling tube, and a pencil and notebook.

How to take the samples

Sampling methods differ, depending on whether you use a shovel, trowel, or soil sampling tube, but the principles remain the same. From the Auburn University Extension Service in Alabama comes this advice on taking soil samples:

Using a garden trowel. "Dig a hole 6 inches deep (2 inches deep on established sods). Start at the bottom of the hole and collect soil by bringing the trowel up the side of the hole to the surface. Take soil from at least five holes to make up one sample; scrape off about 4 tablespoons of soil from the side of each hole (20 tablespoons will fill a pint carton).

"If you are sampling larger areas, take soil from more holes but less soil from each hole, so you can still get it in one carton.

Using a shovel and tablespoon. "Push shovel 6 to 7 inches deep into the soil. Then push handle forward, with shovel still in soil, to make an opening wide enough to start at the bottom of the hole (2 inches from the surface on sod areas) and scrape soil from the side with the tablespoon. After the soil is taken, remove the shovel, let the soil fall back in place and step on it to make it firm. Scrape just enough soil from the holes in the sampling area to fill the pint box (about 20 tablespoons). This method is very good in flower beds, around shrubbery, or in lawns where you don't want to disturb the surface any more than necessary.

Using a soil tube. "Push the tube into the soil about 6 inches deep (2 inches on sods) for the sample. Drop the soil collected in the probe into a clean bucket. [Note: It is best to use a clean *plastic* bucket

or container to collect the individual cores, especially if micronutrients are to be determined in the test. Metal containers, such as galvanized buckets, will contaminate the soil sample with elements such as zinc and copper, and give misleading results.] When soil is collected from various points, mix and put it in your pint carton.

"Label each pint sample carton and record this information (name or number) on the information sheet that goes to the laboratory. Put this information in your notebook, also, to have a record for use when you get the report back from the laboratory.

Flower beds. "Make three separate holes in different places for areas 100 square feet or smaller.

"When sampling an area larger than 100 square feet, make more holes and take less soil from each hole so that the pint container will be just filled when equal amounts of soil from each hole are combined.

Around shrubs and trees. "Take soil from several holes around shrubs at the edge of the branch spread. If only one or two plants are involved, get soil from at least three holes for each shrub or tree. For a large tree, soil from eight to ten spots may be needed for one sample. If several shrubs are in a group, get soil from one hole by each.

Lawns. "For established turf on small areas, take soil from the top 2 [to 6] inches at ten or more places for the sample. If there is a big difference in soil conditions, sample each area separately. For example, part of an area may be filled and part may be excavated into the subsoil. Thus, a soil sample would be needed from each part the first time a soil test is made.

"If turf is not yet established, take soil from the top 5-6 inches in at least ten holes to represent the area sample.

Small vegetable garden. "Take soil from ten holes, 5-6 inches deep, in small vegetable gardens.

Your notebook. "Don't trust your memory. Record each sample in your notebook; assign it a number and describe the plants and location and date. Then you can identify each sample when the laboratory report is received."

Soil Samples
EQUIPMENT NEEDED

Plastic bucket

Soil probe or . . .

Shovel and tablespoon or . . .

Trowel

With a **Soil Probe:** Push the proble into the soil to the depth required. 6-8 inches in garden soil; 2-6 inches in sod. Pull it out and tap the sample into the bucket.

With a **Shovel & Tablespoon:** Push the shovel into the soil and push the handle forward to open a wedge-shaped hole. Scrape the sample from the side of the hole with the spoon—one stroke, bottom to top.

With a **Trowel:** Dig a small hole, then scrape soil from the side of the hole—one stroke, bottom to top. Start scraping 6-8 inches deep in garden soil; 2-6 inches in sod.

WHERE TO DIG

Lawns: Take soil from 10 or more holes for a sample. For a new lawn take soil from the top 5 or 6 inches of soil; for an established lawn, take samples from the top 2-6 inches of soil.

Trees or Shrubs: Take soil from 6-8-inch deep holes around the drip line. If only one or two plants are involved, get soil from at least 3 holes by each. If several plants are involved, get soil from one hole by each.

Flower Beds: Take soil from at least 3 or 4 holes in each 100 square foot area, 6-8 inches or so deep. Make separate samples for each area where conditions are different (see text).

Vegetable Gardens: Take soil from 10 or more holes, 6-8 inches deep.

HOW TO SHIP

Some Extension Agents and soil laboratories have special sample boxes and shipping cartons along with their own instructions for taking and sending samples. If these are provided to you follow them faithfully. If not, collect soil as outlined above . . .

Put the soil from the holes in one area only into the plastic bucket and mix it.

Put 2 cups of this mixture into a plastic bag, fold a few times and

secure it with a rubber band. Put the soil sample along with an infor-

mation sheet (see text) into a strong mailing envelope and ship.

How to Read a Soil Test Report

There is no one standardized format for all soil test reports, but most labs furnish information in the same general categories: **soil texture, pH, and soil fertility.** The fertility is most commonly expressed as the amounts of nitrogen, phosphorus and potassium present in the sample (some labs will indicate the levels of the secondary micronutrients, as well —see pages 49 to 53). Labs in some areas will include the **electrical conductivity** (EC) of the soil, which measures the total salts present. Some labs will also report the total amount of **lime** in the soil.

The illustration below is a composite of many laboratories' forms, so don't be surprised if your own report isn't an exact duplicate. The following information will help you to interpret the lab's analysis.

Texture

The texture of the soil is usually indicated as one of the following: sand, loamy sand, sandy loam, loam, silt loam, silty clay loam, sandy clay loam, clay loam, sandy clay, silty clay, or clay. These classifications can be, for general purposes, broken into three categories and described as having the following characteristics:

Sand Loamy sand	Sandy loam Loam Silt loam Silty clay loam Sandy clay loam Clay loam	Sandy clay Silty clay Clay
Sandy soils: Coarse textured, low water retention, infertile; fertilizer leaches easily; needs frequent irrigation. Adding organic matter helps retain water and nutrients.	**Loam soils:** Have desirable properties of clay and sand, good moisture and fertilizer retention, good workability.	**Clayey soils:** Sticky; high water retention, slow water penetration; compacts easily, and has high fertilizer retention. Needs organic matter to keep it workable.

Lime

In the few areas where soils are naturally calcareos, high or moderate levels of solid lime in the soil may aggravate "lime-induced iron-chlorosis" in susceptible plants (the acid-lovers, primarily). The test determines the amount of solid lime distributed in the soil. If this test is performed, the lab will usually indicate the level of lime using one of three designations: high, moderate, and none or slight. In other areas, where the soil is naturally on the acid side, gardeners may want to add lime. See pH.

If you take soil samples from more than one area, it's a good idea to number your samples and record the information in a notebook at home. When the report is returned, check your notes to make sure the results refer to the proper area.

Lab No. _____
Date _____
Name _____
Address _____
City, State, Zip _____

Results of Soil Analysis

SAMPLE NO.

Comments _____

Electrical conductivity

The electrical conductivity of a saturated sample of soil is a measure of the total salts in the soil. This can be related to plant growth as follows:

0 to 2   No damage to plants

2 to 4   Sensitive plants may be affected adversely

4 to 8   Many plants affected

pH

Normal pH levels of garden soils vary between 4.5 and 8.0. If your sample has a pH reading of between 6.1 and 7.5, most garden plants will perform satisfactorily, except certain of the acid-loving plants. To lower soil pH, use soil sulfur, another acid-forming chemical or an acid-forming mulch. To raise the pH, use lime at the recommended amounts. For the complete story of soil pH, see page 26.

Soil fertility

The amounts of nitrogen, phosphorus and potassium (N, P and K, respectively) will be expressed in units indicating parts per million (ppm) in dry soil, and fall into three categories:

	Low	Medium	High
N:	0 to 20	20 to 50	over 50
P:	0 to 12	12 to 25	over 25
K:	0 to 50	50 to 100	over 100

Note: The numerical distinctions are not necessarily hard and fast indicators of high, medium and low levels of fertility for all plants. The numbers were arrived at using a limited number of test plants, and are generally considered to be average figures. Therefore test results may indicate low levels of fertility even though the plants in your garden are flourishing. This is possible because the nutrient needs of many plants are not "average."

Low levels: Definite need for fertilizer nutrients. Add nutrients at recommended rate for plant and soil in question.

Medium levels: Fertilizer nutrients are present in adequate amounts. Maintain present program.

High levels: There is no need for adding fertilizer nutrients at this time, except in special starter applications.

SOIL ANALYSIS REPORT FORM

DESCRIPTION OF SOIL AREA	TEXTURE	LIME	pH	EC	N	P	K

Where to Write For Soil Tests

ALABAMA
Soil Testing Laboratory
Auburn University
Auburn, Alabama 36830

ALASKA
Palmer Plant and Soils
  Analysis Laboratory
Agricultural Experiment Station
Palmer Research Center
P.O. Box AE
Palmer, Alaska 99645

ARIZONA
Soil, Water, and Plant Tissue
Testing Laboratory
Department of Soils, Water and
Engineering
University of Arizona
Tucson, Arizona 85721

ARKANSAS
Contact your County Extension
Agent, or write:
Soil Testing Laboratory
Cooperative Extension Service
1201 McAlmont
P.O. Box 391
Little Rock, Arkansas 72203

CALIFORNIA
Soil testing is not provided by
the state but there are many
commercial soil laboratories.
Check your telephone directory
or with your County Extension
Agent.

COLORADO
Contact your County Extension
Agent, or write:
Soil Testing Laboratory
Colorado State University
Fort Collins, Colorado 80523

CONNECTICUT
Agronomy Section
College of Agriculture and
Natural Resources
The University of Connecticut
Storrs, Connecticut 06268

Soil Testing Service
District Office, Cooperative
Extension Service
(check telephone directory)

DELAWARE
Soil Testing Laboratory
University of Delaware
Newark, Delaware 19711

FLORIDA
Contact your County Extension
Agent, or write:
Soil Testing Laboratory
University of Florida
Gainesville, Florida 32601

GEORGIA
Soil Testing and Plant Analysis
Laboratory
2400 College Station Road
Athens, Georgia 30601

HAWAII
Soil Testing Service
Cooperative Extension Service
University of Hawaii
Honolulu, Hawaii 96822

IDAHO
Contact your County Extension
Agent, or write:
Soil Testing Laboratory
Department of Plant &
Soil Science
College of Agriculture
Moscow, Idaho 83843

ILLINOIS
Soil testing is not offered by
any public agency in Illinois.
Check the telephone directory
for private laboratories.

INDIANA
Plant and Soil Analysis
Laboratory
Life Science Building
Purdue University
West Lafayette, Indiana 47907

IOWA
Soil Testing Laboratory
Cooperative Extension Service
Iowa State University
Ames, Iowa 50010

KANSAS
Contact your County Extension
Agent, or write:
Agronomy Department
Kansas State University
Manhattan, Kansas 66506

KENTUCKY
Soil Testing Laboratory
University of Kentucky
Lexington, Kentucky 40506

LOUISIANA
Soil Testing Laboratory
Department of Agronomy
Louisiana State University
Baton Rouge, Louisiana 70803

MAINE
Maine Soil Testing Service
25 Deering Hall
University of Maine
Orono, Maine 04473

MARYLAND
United States Department
of Agriculture
Beltsville, Maryland 20705
(for Washington D.C. residents)

University of Maryland
Soil Testing Laboratory
College Park, Maryland 20742

MASSACHUSETTS
Soil Testing Service
Department of Plant and Soil
Sciences
Stockbridge Hall
University of Massachusetts
Amherst, Massachusetts 01003

MICHIGAN
Crop and Soil Sciences
Department
Michigan State University
East Lansing, Michigan 48824

MINNESOTA
Soil Testing Laboratory
University of Minnesota
St. Paul, Minnesota 55108

MISSISSIPPI
Contact your County Extension
Agent, or write:
Soil Testing
Box 5405
Mississippi State University
Oxford, Mississippi 39762

MISSOURI
Soil Testing Laboratory
University of Missouri
Columbia, Missouri 65201

MONTANA
Soil Testing Laboratory
Plant and Soil Science
Department
Montana State University
Bozeman, Montana 59715

NEBRASKA
Contact your County Extension Agent, or write:
Soil Testing Laboratory
University of Nebraska—Lincoln
Department of Agronomy
Keim Hall, East Campus
Lincoln, Nebraska 68503

NEVADA
Contact your County Extension Agent, or write:
Nevada Soil and Water Testing Laboratory
College of Agriculture
University of Nevada
Reno, Nevada 89507

NEW HAMPSHIRE
University of New Hampshire
Analytical Services Department
Durham, New Hampshire 03824

NEW JERSEY
Soil Testing Laboratory
Cook College
Rutgers University
New Brunswick, New Jersey 08903

NEW MEXICO
New Mexico State University
Soil, Plant, and Water Testing Laboratory
Agronomy Department,
P.O. Box 3Q
Las Cruces, New Mexico 88003

NEW YORK
Contact your County Extension Agent, or write:
Agronomy Department
804 Bradfield Hall
Cornell University
Ithaca, New York 14853

NORTH CAROLINA
Contact your County Extension Agent for mailing kits and directions, or write:
Agronomic Division
North Carolina Department of Agriculture
Raleigh, North Carolina 27611

NORTH DAKOTA
Soil Testing Laboratory
Waldron Hall
North Dakota State University
Fargo, North Dakota 58102

OKLAHOMA
Contact your County Extension Agent, or write:
Soil Testing Laboratory
Agronomy Department
Oklahoma State University
Stillwater, Oklahoma 74074

OHIO
Cooperative Extension Office
Ohio State University
2120 Fyffe Road
Columbus, Ohio 43210

OREGON
Soil Testing Laboratory
Oregon State University
Corvalis, Oregon 97331

PENNSYLVANIA
Contact your County Extension Agent, or write:
School of Agriculture
Pennsylvania State University
University Park,
Pennsylvania 16802

RHODE ISLAND
Soil Testing Laboratory
Plant Science Greenhouse
University of Rhode Island
Kingston, Rhode Island 02881

SOUTH CAROLINA
Sample boxes and record sheets are available from your County Extension Agent's office, or write:
Soil Testing Laboratory
Clemson University
Clemson, South Carolina 29631

SOUTH DAKOTA
Soil Testing Laboratory
South Dakota State University
Brookings, South Dakota 57007

TENNESSEE
Soil Testing Laboratory
University of Tennessee
P.O. Box 11019
Nashville, Tennessee 37211

TEXAS
Texas Agricultural Extension Service
The Texas A&M University System
Soil Testing Laboratory
College Station, Texas 77843

UTAH
Soil, Plant, and Water Analysis Laboratory
Utah State University, UMC 48
Logan, Utah 84322

VERMONT
Soil Testing Laboratory
Regulatory Services
University of Vermont
Burlington, Vermont 05401

VIRGINIA
Contact your County or City Extension Agent, or write:
Soil Testing Laboratory
Cooperative Extension Service
Virginia Polytechnic Institute and State University
Blacksburg, Virginia 24061

WASHINGTON
Soil Testing Laboratory
Washington State University
Pullman, Washington 99163

WEST VIRGINIA
Soil Testing Laboratory
West Virginia University
Morgantown, West Virginia 26506

WISCONSIN
Soil and Plant Analysis Laboratory
University of Wisconsin
806 S. Park Street
Madison, Wisconsin 53715, or,

State Soils Laboratory
Route 2
Marshfield, Wisconsin 54449

WYOMING
Soil Testing Laboratory
Plant Science Division
University of Wyoming
Box 3354, University Station
Laramie, Wyoming 82071

CANADA
Soil and Feed Testing Laboratory
University of Alberta
O.S. Longman Building
6909 116 Street
Edmonton, Alberta, or,

Soil Testing Unit
British Columbia Department of Agriculture
1873 Small Road
Kelowna, British Columbia
V1Y 4R2

Soil pH

The subject of soil pH as it relates to growing plants can be as simple or complicated as you care to make it. In the old days, a seasoned gardener would call an acid soil "sour" and add ground chalk or marl (a limey clay) to correct the condition. Highly alkaline soils were best left unfarmed, but a moderately alkaline soil could be improved with the addition of organic matter that was known to be acid, such as pine needles or certain peats. As far as today's gardener is concerned, the technology may be more sophisticated but the basics remain the same.

Why is pH important?
It really isn't enough just to say that the proper pH is important for good plant growth—why is it important? That's not a mystery: the pH of soil affects plant growth in four important ways: (1) It has a distinct effect on the availability of essential nutrients—(see chart, below). (2) It has an effect on soil microorganisms: the optimum pH range for soil-borne bacteria is between 5.4 and 8. (3) It has a direct effect on root cells that in turn affect the root's ability to absorb both nutrients and water. (4) It has an effect on the solubility of toxic substances.

The pH scale
The pH scale is traditionally presented as a numerical chart (see illustration, below) and is used to indicate the relative acidity or alkalinity of a given substance. The scale runs from 0 (extremely acid) to 14 (extremely alkaline). The middle of the scale (pH reading of 7) is the neutral point. By itself, it is a simple concept but what confuses many gardeners is that the pH scale is not a simple arithmetic series, but rather a logarithmic function. Therefore, each pH unit represents a tenfold increase or decrease in relative acidity or alkalinity. For example, a soil with a pH of 6.0 is 10 times more acid that one with a pH of 7.0. Similarly, a soil of 8.0 is 10 times more alkaline than one with a pH of 7.0, and 100 times more alkaline than one with a pH of 6.0.

But what do you, as a gardener, really need to know about soil pH? Three things: how to find out the pH of your own soil, what the optimum pH is for the plants you care to grow, and how to correct an overly acid or alkaline condition.

If you have your soil tested at a professional laboratory, the pH reading will automatically be included in your report. If you do not have a soil test made, you can determine the pH of your soil using a commercial kit, available through scientific supply stores or catalogs.

Garden vegetables, most of the common annual flowers, most lawn grasses, and many perennials and shrubs do best in slightly to very slightly acid soil—down to about 6. The pH of the average garden soil falls somewhere between 4.5 and 7, and above 7 in much of the arid West.

Acid soils. These are common in areas of heavy rainfall, occurring often in the Pacific Northwest and the Eastern seaboard. In these and certain other areas, accumulated rainfall has been sufficient to leach

Soil Reaction Chart (pH)

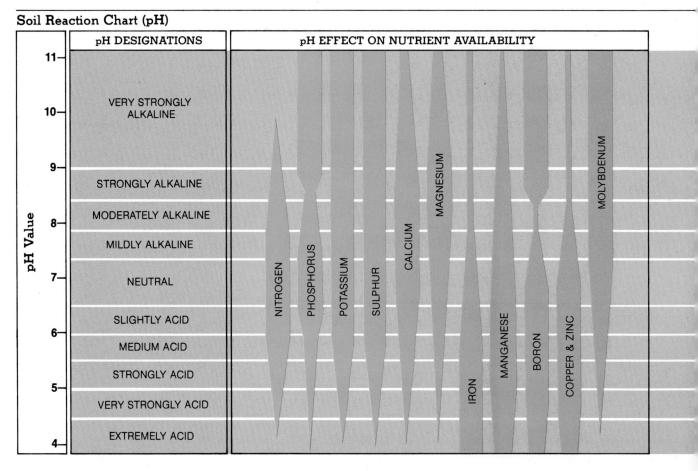

the naturally-occurring alkali chemical elements (calcium, magnesium, sodium, potassium) from the soil, leaving behind a disproportionate amount of the acidic elements.

If a pH test indicates your soil is too acid—a pH of 6.0 or below—the most common cure is to "lime" the soil.

There are many kinds of liming materials but the best is *finely ground* dolomitic limestone (sometimes called magnesic limestone). Dolomitic limestone is different from common limestone in that it contains both magnesium carbonate and calcium carbonate, whereas common limestone has no magnesium carbonate.

Soils that need to be limed are frequently deficient in both calcium and magnesium, both of which are essential plant nutrients, so using this product makes good sense.

There is no hard-and-fast formula for rates of application suitable to all soils. The rate depends on the quantity of clay and organic matter in the soil: the heavier the soil, the more lime you need.

The following are rule-of-thumb rates of application for various soils in the northern and central states: To increase the pH by one unit, for each 1,000 square feet of area to be treated, add:

35 pounds of fine limestone for very sandy soils,
50 pounds of fine limestone for sandy soils,
70 pounds of fine limestone for loams,
80 pounds of fine limestone for loamy clays and clays.

In the southern and coastal states, reduce the application by approximately one-half.

Remember, too, that the effects of liming are not permanent. Reapplication should be made every two or three years, after checking the pH level.

Alkaline soils. The most common and extreme alkali soils occur in arid desert regions. An overabundance of alkaline substances such as calcium and sodium makes the soil alkaline.

If your soil is moderately or mildly alkaline, ordinary powdered sulfur or an acid mulch (pine needles, sawdust or acid peat) will help correct the condition. Ammonium-containing fertilizers, such as ammonium sulfate, tend to leave an acid reaction and should be favored over other fertilizers to lower soil pH.

If sulfur is needed to reduce alkalinity, the rates of application will depend on the type of soil you have and its original pH. Given the information in a soil test report, your county extension agent or local nursery will be able to recommend the proper amounts of sulfur to apply.

In areas of extremely alkaline soils, the best answer for the gardener would be to concentrate on gardening in containers and raised beds (see page 42) filled with a synthetic soil mix.

Notable exceptions
Although it is true that most plants will grow well in soils having a pH between 6 and 7.5, there are exceptions. There is a whole group of plants known collectively as the "acid-lovers" that require a soil pH of between 4.5 and 5.5. Acid-lovers include: camellias, azaleas, rhododendrons, pieris, ternstroemia, hydrangeas, blueberries and others. For more about specific plants, read Special Handling, page 85.

Soil Reaction Chart (pH)

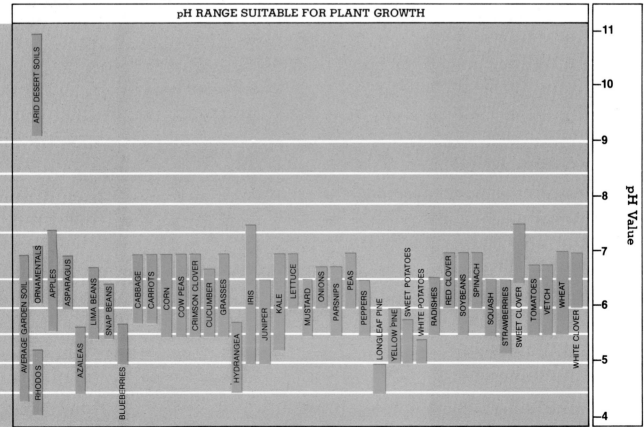

Soil Pests

We wish we could pass on some magical method of controlling small field animals, but unfortunately that isn't the case.

Gophers and moles present a real problem to gardeners in many areas of the country. How can you tell whether it's a gopher or a mole causing the damage? A gopher eats roots, including bulbs, tubers, roots of trees, vines and shrubs; and occasionally whole plants disappear into his hole. Gophers tunnel from 6 to 12 inches under the soil and push the excavated dirt out to the surface, leaving small mounds of fine-particled earth. The mounds are not completely symmetrical.

The mole is considered to be insectivorous, eating larvae and worms, and occasionally tulip bulbs. The mole burrows so close to the soil surface that you can plainly see his route. In the tunnel-making process, moles break off tender root systems, snap stems, and uproot seedlings. Molehills are symmetrical, and look like small volcanoes. Unlike the gopher's pulverized soil, the soil that makes up a molehill is in small compact plugs.

Down through gardening history have come many tried-and-not-so-true instructions for the eradication of these animals. For instance, you can put a garden hose into one of the runways and flood them out; this is of dubious value at best, and it is an incredible waste of water. Or you might attach a garden hose to the tail pipe of an operating car, and gas the devils out with carbon monoxide—which seems a classic case of the cure being more trouble than the ailment. There are any number of traps, some of which claim high success rates (ask at your local nursery and follow the manufacturer's instructions carefully).

Commercially available poison grains are occasionally effective.

And there are gas bombs that you light and stick into the hole. Or you may plant rows of "mole plant" (*Euphorbia lathyris*) around the perimeter of your garden, because the roots and stems of *Euphorbia lathyris* contain a caustic poison that may, or may not, repel subterranean invaders. And finally, there is the organized and studied placement of wooden windmills called "Klippety-Klops" that send vibrations down into the soil and reportedly scare moles and gophers away.

All of this would begin to take on a comical quality if the damage done by gophers and moles wasn't so infuriating to gardeners, particularly when the creatures seem to outsmart the most diligent efforts to get rid of them.

Last-straw controls include two of the more direct and unquestionably effective methods. One is to wait silently for hours over a new tunnel or hill for the creature to stick its unsuspecting head out, then whack it with a shovel or let

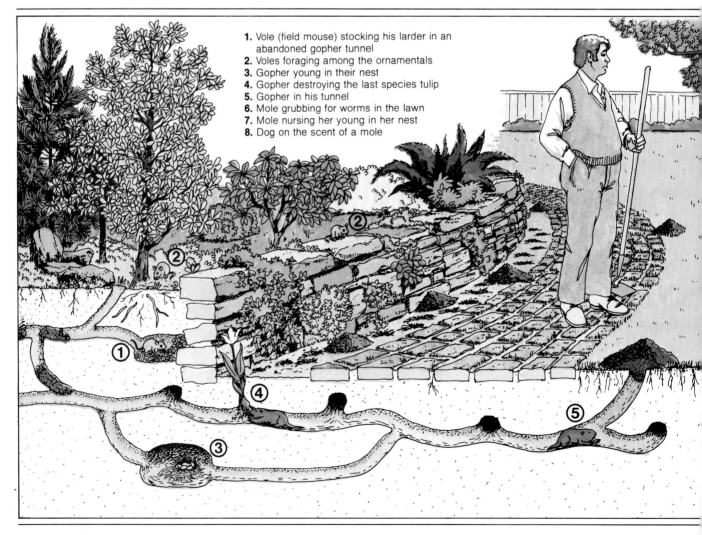

1. Vole (field mouse) stocking his larder in an abandoned gopher tunnel
2. Voles foraging among the ornamentals
3. Gopher young in their nest
4. Gopher destroying the last species tulip
5. Gopher in his tunnel
6. Mole grubbing for worms in the lawn
7. Mole nursing her young in her nest
8. Dog on the scent of a mole

go with a blast from a shotgun. Local ordinances rarely allow the use of a gun within city limits, but we know of more than a few country gophers who have met their reward this way.

In practice, there seems to be only one surefire, albeit limited method to control gophers and moles. It falls into the "preventative measures" category. If you've decided that raised beds (page 42) are for you, you can avoid all gopher and mole attacks in this defined area by lining the bed with ½-inch mesh wire before you fill the bed with soil. This is a particularly good idea for protecting expensive spring-flowering bulbs. For individual plants, shrubs, prized specimens and the like, you can avoid damage using the same technique: line the planting hole with 1-inch mesh wire.

Field mice and voles. These varmints are less of a problem. They may be as hard to eradicate as gophers and moles—in whose abandoned tunnels they often live

A collection of some of the time-honored methods of gopher and mole eradication tells the story of the frustration felt by gardeners when these pests enter the garden.

—but their damage is easier to prevent. Instead of attacking plants underground, voles and field mice, and occasionally rabbits and porcupines, attack the aboveground portion of plants. They often "girdle" the base of trees and shrubs —gnaw the bark from around

them. If enough bark is removed, the tree will die with the first surge of spring growth. Protect the lower trunk, particularly in winter when attacks are common, with a cylinder of hardware cloth. Check occasionally to be sure it doesn't become too tight as the tree grows.

Mulches and Amendments

Mulching is one of gardening's oldest techniques. The English word was probably derived from the German vernacular, *molsch,* meaning soft and rotten. It is probable that mulch in olden days was usually a litter of straw that farmers and gardeners realized would keep the soil cool and moist.

Until fairly recently, the types of mulch used were all natural. In the past few years, university researchers, commercial farmers and home gardeners have experimented with black and clear polyethylene film as mulches, and have achieved good results. Natural and manmade mulches have their unique advantages and drawbacks—it's up to the gardener to decide which is better in the given situation.

The plastic mulches may have great advantages in increasing crop yields and in weed control, but their virtues in no way deny the value of a natural organic mulch.

---

1. A heavy layer of straw mulch, applied before the first winter snows, will keep the soil from freezing and make it easy to dig root crops—built-in cold-storage.

2. In our own test gardens we experimented with grape pomace as a soil amendment, and the leftover stems as a surface for pathways. The results were encouraging.

3. When you add an amendment to the soil, the amount you add must be enough to physically change the structure of the soil. One-third to one-half of the final mix should be organic matter. This means if you plan to incorporate the amendment into the soil to a depth of 12 inches, the layer of organic matter should be 4-6 inches deep.

4. Mini raised beds covered with black plastic hastened the maturity of this strawberry crop. Medium-sized redwood bark covers the walkways between the rows.

What's the difference?

The gallery of organic substances pictured on pages 32 to 35 includes many materials commonly used as both mulches and soil amendments. The difference between a soil amendment and a mulch is not in the nature of the material but in the method of application: a soil amendment is incorporated *into* the soil, using a tiller or spade, to improve the soil's texture and structure. A mulch is applied in a fairly thick layer *on top of* the soil, and although it performs many of the functions of an amendment, an application of mulch has a number of other positive effects.

Natural Mulches

In the garden, natural or "organic" mulch will benefit plant growth in many ways and at the same time give the garden a well-groomed look.

Because natural organic mulches are derived from plant material, they decompose and hence affect the soil and plants in several important ways.

Helps granulation. If not too decomposed, the mulch will promote granulation or the clinging together of soil particles. During decomposition of organic matter, soil microorganisms secrete a sticky substance that plays an important role in soil aggregation. Because of the mulch layer, the soil structure (the arrangement of the particles) is not disturbed by pelting rains or overhead irrigation. Cultivating the soil when it is too wet destroys good soil structure. But when mulches are used, little or no cultivation is necessary.

Remember that the values of organic mulches are summertime values—reducing soil temperatures and holding moisture. The vegetable gardener should be particularly aware that laying down an organic mulch in early spring will slow up the natural warming of the soil as spring advances, pushing the planting date farther on. As an insulating blanket, a mulch reduces solar radiation into the soil. As a result, frost hazards are greater in a mulched bed. Gardeners sometimes disagree on the time to apply mulches (there are those who leave a thick layer over the garden area the year round), but our experience tells us to wait until the soil is thoroughly warmed before applying a mulch.

Stops crusting. If you find yourself having to break up a crust on the soil surface after a rain or after watering, then you need to apply a mulch. Raindrops do a cementing job by packing the small soil particles between the larger ones so that the pores are plugged and no more water can enter. A mulch diffuses the impact of the water drops, and the soil pores remain open.

A mulch beneath unstaked tomatoes, summer squash, cucumbers or strawberries lessens the loss of fruit through rot. A tomato sitting on damp soil invites the soil bacteria to do their normal thing. And muddy splashes from rain may start rot in lettuce.

Controls weeds. For weed control the mulch must be thick enough so that weed seedlings can't grow through it on their own stored food. Perennial weeds will thrive in spite of organic mulches, or because of them. Black plastic (see page 36) will take care of all kinds of weeds and grasses, and it can be used under any of the other mulches.

Conserves moisture. Mulches slow down the evaporation of water from the upper 6 to 8 inches of soil. Tests show that merely shading the bare soil will reduce evaporation as much as 30 percent but a straw mulch, for example, will reduce evaporation as much as 70 percent.

A mulch not only saves water but it helps maintain an even supply of moisture in the upper layers of the soil.

Protects riches. By insulating the top few inches of the soil from the sun's heat and by maintaining soil moisture up to the surface, a mulch gives the roots a free run in the richest layers of the soil. Tests show that a plant's main root under mulch grows as deeply as under bare soil. The additional surface roots are the bonus a mulch gives.

How thick a mulch? Fine grained organic mulches such as sawdust should be applied 1 to 2 inches thick. Coarse or fluffy materials can be applied 3 to 4 inches thick. Materials such as straw or chopped corncobs may be covered with a more attractive mulch.

Apply mulch evenly. When using a mulch that becomes soggy when wet, don't pack it around the stem or trunk of the plant. If a mulch is thoroughly wet, pull it back a few inches from the stem or trunk so that air can circulate freely to the base of the plant.

A mulch should be maintained at its original thickness. As it thins down, add new material. As the mulch decomposes or is washed into the soil, the structure of the soil is gradually improved. After a few years of regular additions of organic mulches, you should have a very fine garden soil to work in.

Note: Soil bacteria go to work on the sawdust and take the nitrogen they need from the soil, in effect robbing it from the plants. But the loss is not as great as when sawdust is mixed in with the soil. A good rule of thumb is to increase the amount of nitrogen fertilizer regularly used for the crop by one-quarter when using a sawdust mulch.

An Array of Amendments and Mulches

On the next four pages, we take a look at a wide variety of soil amendments and mulches. Because some of these materials are by-products of regional industries, they may not be available in your area. Remember to follow one general rule when applying organic amendments: don't skimp. In almost every case, the more you apply, the better the soil will be.

Fir bark
Available in a wide variety of sizes for use as a mulch or soil amendment. Some gardeners prefer ground fir bark, as opposed to redwood bark, for use in container soil mixes. Most products have been nitrogen-stabilized. When used as a mulch, fir bark will weather to an attractive silver grey color.

Chunk bark
Redwood and fir are the most popular forms of chunk bark available. The bark normally comes in three different sizes: fine, medium and large. The larger the size of the chunk, the longer it takes to decompose; even the finest grade may take more than one season to break down. Redwood bark is reddish brown when first applied, then gradually weathers to brownish gray. It has a pleasant odor.

Chipper material
As more communities limit the amount of burning allowed, more garden refuse is put through a chipper. The resulting product can be composted, used as an amendment, mulch, or as a material for garden walkways. The rate of decomposition depends on the original material chipped: hardwoods take longer to decompose than softwoods. Extra nitrogen should be applied if this material is used as an amendment, to compensate for "nitrogen pull."

Compost
You can make at home an excellent soil amendment and mulch by composting various kinds of nonwoody plant refuse such as grass clippings, leaves and plant tops from the vegetable and flower garden. When partially decomposed, this material rates as one of the best organic mulches, although it may not be the most attractive. See pages 46 to 47 for instructions on making your own compost and page 57 for a discussion on compost as fertilizer.

Sand
There are many kinds of sand available, but for gardening use, washed and screened quartz sand is superior. The coarser products should be favored for their aerating qualities. Unscreened sand will contain a range of particle sizes and not aerify as well. Sand is commonly used as a component of container soil mixes, for rooting cuttings, and occasionally used in very large quantities to modify the texture of clay soils. The quantities needed for such an operation put sand as a soil amendment out of the range of most home gardeners.

Buying organic soil amendments in bulk makes good sense and saves money if: you have a large area you're going to cover with a mulch, you're amending the soil in a good-sized garden plot, or are mixing your own synthetic soil mix in large quantities.

Hay

Hay is used mostly in farm gardens, since it is the material most likely to be available. No additional nitrogen is necessary. Because of its light weight, hay will blow in the wind.

Bagasse

A by-product of the manufacture of sugar, this material is actually spent, dried, sugar cane. Naturally its availability is somewhat geographically limited, but it is becoming increasingly available outside of sugar producing regions. Bagasse is somewhat acidic in reaction (similar to Canadian peat moss) and has a high water-holding capacity. Used both as an amendment and a mulch.

Lawn clippings

This material is best when used dry. If applied fresh, it should be spread loosely on the surface of the soil. Otherwise, it mats down, produces heat during decomposition and gives off an offensive odor. Do not use grass clippings if the lawn has been treated with a weed killer. Thatch removed from a lawn can also be used as an amendment or mulch. Do not use thatch which contains Bermuda grass, unless you want it to grow wherever you spread the thatch.

A deep layer of straw keeps the soil cool for good lettuce production. Make sure the straw is seed-free or you'll have a problem with weeds.

Leaf mold

Leaves that are composted in the fall of the year should, if properly handled, be partially decomposed and ready for use by spring. Leaf mold is a particularly good mulch for many of the acid-loving plants, such as azaleas and rhododendrons, and some ferns. When used as a topdressing, it may be somewhat difficult to spread evenly.

Strawy manure

Manure makes an excellent mulch or soil amendment if you don't mind the odor for the first couple of days. Manure should be partially decomposed because fresh manure can burn tender roots. Be sure that it hasn't been treated with odor-reducing chemicals, which are sometimes injurious to growing plants. No nitrogen needs to be added with manure.

Mushroom compost

This material is often available in areas where mushrooms are produced commercially. It is usually inexpensive and has a good color that blends into the landscape. It's often available by the bagful, and sometimes by the cubic yard in large garden supply stores. Unleached mushroom compost may contain toxic levels of accumulated salt. Incorporate no more than 50 percent by volume in the soil if used as an amendment.

Peat moss

This is one of the most commonly used amendments and is an essential ingredient in many synthetic soil formulas (see page 40). As a topdressing it is quite rich looking. But the cost of peat moss is often prohibitive when large areas are to be covered. Various particle sizes are available. Many commercial growers of acid-loving plants use straight peat moss as a planting medium. When very dry, peat sheds water rather than allowing it to soak in.

Pine needles

This material makes a light, porous, attractive mulch. Since pine needles are moderately acid, they are especially desirable for acid-loving plants such as azaleas and blueberries.

Pomace (apple or grape)

Pomace is the spent seeds and skins of apples and grapes— a by-product of cider and winery operations. If you're lucky enough to live in an area where these products are produced, you should take advantage of their special properties. Studies of grape pomace have shown it to be a slow-to-decompose soil amendment that releases small quantities of nitrogen to the soil over a sustained period of time. It is good for modifying clay soils. The odor may be somewhat heady for the first couple of weeks.

Poultry litter

In many areas, this material is available from poultry farms. The litter material may be straw, sawdust, crushed corncobs, wood chips or some other organic material. The poultry manure mixed with the litter takes care of nitrogen requirements. Apply this material sparingly until you know how much to use without damaging plants from an overdose of fertilizer.

Sawdust

This is a very common mulch material in areas where it is readily available. But a nitrogen deficiency almost inevitably occurs in the soil after applying unfortified sawdust— unless applications of nitrogen fertilizer are made regularly. Reports of toxic materials in sawdust have not been substantiated by research.

Straw

Used primarily for winter protection, straw can also be used as a summer mulch to cool soils. It is not the most attractive mulch and should be regarded as highly flammable. It should not be used where a cigarette could be carelessly dropped into it. Unless you want a good crop of oats, avoid using oat straw as a mulch.

Redwood soil conditioner

This is a popular material, used primarily as a soil amendment. A direct by-product of the lumber industry, this product is usually nitrogen-fortified and composted for 3-4 months at the mill. Redwood soil conditioner is an extremely long-lasting organic material, and has been shown to last in the soil for as long as ten years.

Manmade Mulches

Manmade mulches include such material as black, clear and sky-blue polyethylene film, aluminum foil, paper coated with aluminum foil, biodegradable paper and some experimental degradable plastic mulches. Not all of these mulches are popular enough to be commercially available; the most common manmade mulches used by home gardeners are black and clear plastic film. Both are frequently available in rolls at larger nurseries and garden supply centers.

Plastic mulches have pronounced effects on the soil they cover, and ultimately on the plants grown. But there are considerable differences in the way black and clear plastic deal with the sun.

The sun's rays that reach the earth are absorbed or reflected back, depending on what kind of surface they fall on. The rays that warm the object they hit are "short" rays. The object reradiates its stored heat but in a different wave length: in "long" rays.

The short rays of the sun travel through glass, translucent paper, clear plastic film and other transparent or translucent materials.

The nature of the mulch determines the input of the heat stored. The clear plastic mulch allows the short rays of the sun to enter the soil and traps heat there, effectively increasing soil temperatures by 10°F or more. A thick layer of organic matter, such as sawdust or other opaque material, reduces the input of heat and has a cooling effect on the soil. A cover of a reflective material, such as aluminum foil or white coated plastic, will reflect the short rays of the sun and drop the soil temperature considerably below that of soil directly exposed to the sun's rays.

Plastic Advantages

The following are some of the claims made for plastic mulches, which we can support after many seasons of experience with them. We do *not* claim that plastic mulches are beautiful to look at, but they can be covered with a good looking topdressing.

Plastic mulches modify soil temperature, conserve soil moisture, control weeds (black plastic), prevent root injury because the soil is not cultivated, maintain good soil structure by preventing crusting and compaction of the soil, reflect light that repels certain insects (colored plastics), improve soil moisture-holding capacity and provide for an economical means of water distribution—drip irrigation.

Watering through plastic mulches is not a problem, and gardeners who have drip irrigation systems save water (see page 80 for more about drip irrigation). Other users of plastic mulches cut upside-down T-slits in the plastic for watering with sprinklers, run water through the planting holes, or lay a soaker hose under the plastic.

Black plastic film. The material most often used by home gardeners is black polyethylene film, which is available in rolls 3 or 4 feet wide and 1 or 1.5 mils thick. Although it's true that clear film will warm the soil more than black film, black film prevents weeds from growing under it because it excludes the light needed for their growth.

A mulch of black plastic film has built itself a solid reputation

How to install plastic mulches

These photos (a collection from various university experiment stations) show a step-by-step procedure in a typical installation of black plastic mulch.

1. A shallow furrow or trench is dug on each side of the row the approximate width of the plastic.

2. Secure end of plastic at end of row.

3. The plastic is rolled out evenly along the row. Edges of plastic are secured by burying them in a trench and covering with soil.

4. A "bulb-planter" is an excellent tool to cut plastic and dig small hole for transplant. Edges of the tool should be sharpened with a file. Cutting a cross-shaped slit in the plastic and manually digging a small hole is an effective alternate, but not as fast. Size of slit will depend on the size of root ball you intend to plant.

5. Here a finished planting hole awaits a transplant in a Jiffy 7 pellet. In hard soil a small amount of soil substitute can be used in hole to give transplants root system a good start.

6. Transplant as usual.

·7. The look of the planted row. Watering the trench on either side of the row works. Side seepage irrigates the row.

8. Properly done the results should look like this.

for increasing yields and speeding up the ripening of melons, eggplant, peppers and summer squash. In areas where temperatures early in the growing season are less than ideal for these warm weather crops, yields of muskmelon in experimental plots have been increased fourfold over the yields of nonmulched plants.

The increase in soil temperature is usually given the credit for the remarkable speedup of growth. However, temperature readings show that the increase is generally only about 3°F to 6°F, and sometimes only 2°F.

The temperature of the film itself soars on a warm sunny day and the film kicks back a great deal of heat to the air above it, rather than transferring it to the soil. The insulating air pockets between the film and the soil surface retard most of the heat transfer from the black plastic to the soil.

Make sure that the soil is damp when the mulch is applied so that there is sufficient moisture for good plant development under the mulch.

Clear plastic film. This has its proponents, too, especially in areas where spring comes late and cool. An agriculture extension agent in the Pacific Northwest experimented with clear plastic film as a mulch and had this to say:

"A layer of clear plastic over the soil aids greatly with warm season crops such as tomatoes, melons, peppers, and all the squash family. The warming of the soil will promote 10 to 14 days earlier maturity and higher yields of tomatoes. Melons, seeded about the 10th of June, gave ripe cantaloupe and watermelon by mid-September.

"We demonstrated that clear plastic is better than black plastic, at least in our cool climate, because the sun's energy is expended on the soil rather than on the top part of the plastic. The weeds were not a major problem under the clear plastic if temperatures of 90°F or more occurred to burn off the weeds. If high temperatures do not occur, the plastic can be lifted, and the weeds pulled by hand."

Home gardeners should also know that a combination of plastic and organic mulches can be very effective. The gardener who uses a plastic mulch to aid in early spring soil warm-up doesn't need to worry if summer temperatures are too hot to keep using plastic. Just add an organic mulch over the top of the plastic to shield it from the direct rays of the sun. In the desert, where summer temperatures of more than 100°F are frequent, black plastic (for weed control) covered with an organic mulch, such as bark chips, is a good growing combination for many plants and shrubs.

Planting in plastic. If you've installed a plastic mulch and the time has come to set out transplants, you may find the job easier if you use a small hand planter. After filing the bottom edge to sharpen it, cut through the mulch cleanly with a twisting motion and continue on to make a planting hole in the soil. The method is simple and avoids unnecessary tearing of the plastic mulch when you try to make a hole by hand. For planting seeds through a plastic mulch, an old-fashioned corn planter (sometimes called a jabber) does a very nice job. Simply push the jabber through the plastic and use it as you would in cultivated soil.

Problem Soils

The most common problem soils are too clayey, too sandy, too shallow, too wet or too saline.

The extremes—clayey and sandy soil. It's well known that clayey and sandy soils present some special problems for the average gardener. Don't interpret this as saying that you cannot have a successful garden in either clayey or sandy soils—you can. But be forewarned: With these soil conditions, there is no real substitute for the knowledge gained by experience. Novice gardeners who don't want to spend the time, effort or money to convert existing clay or sand into a better soil will take some lumps along the way. Success can be had, though, if you're a careful gardener and learn from the successes and failures one year to the next. When it comes time to till, extra care must be taken with clay soils. If tilled when they are too wet, clay soils can become "puddled" (compacted, having no regular structure)—a situation which may take years to reverse. The following advice comes from the Division of Agricultural Sciences at the University of California:

"Clay soils in particular must be handled with great care if favorable results are to be obtained from ordinary tillage practices.

"When moist, clay soils should be dug with a spading fork rather than with a shovel or spade. As the soil is turned over, the large clods should be broken up with the side of the fork. The clods that remain should be exposed to the sun and air. After they have dried and crumbled somewhat, they can be wetted with a fine spray to soften them, and then raked when sufficiently dried again. The combination of air-drying, wetting, and raking will break up most of the clods.

"Although clay soils cannot be made ideal, they can be improved by any treatment which will cause the particles to form small granules and crumbs. The best treatment for this purpose is to incorporate large amounts of organic matter into the soil to promote better soil structure. The

One of the most reliable methods of improving almost any problem soil is the addition of quantities of organic matter. The material can be anything from redwood soil conditioner to poultry litter, and in most cases, the more you add, the better results you'll achieve.

improved condition may remain long after organic matter has disappeared."

The addition of large quantities of organic matter—compost, peat moss, manure, sawdust, ground bark—makes clay soils more mellow and easier to work. Incorporated organic matter opens up tight clay soils, improves drainage and allows air to move more readily through the soil, allowing it to warm earlier in the spring. In sandy soils, organic matter holds moisture and nutrients in the root zone. The more organic matter you add to a sandy soil, the more you increase its capacity to hold moisture and nutrients.

But don't confuse this addition of organic matter to the soil with a long-term improvement program that includes the gradual breakdown of the organic matter into true humus (the black sticky substance that holds soil particles together in aggregates). A soil improvement program is just that —a program—which must be kept up season after season for long-term benefits to accrue.

The quantity of organic matter must be large enough to change the structure of the soil. And enough means that about one-third of the final soil is organic matter. If you are going to "make

loam" 6 inches deep, you will have to spread a layer of organic material over the soil at least 2 inches thick. Add the organic matter when preparing the garden for planting. Spread the normal amount of fertilizer over the organic material and till it into the soil very thoroughly. The normal amount of fertilizer might be 4 to 5 pounds of a 5-10-10 fertilizer per 100 square feet of surface soil.

If you use peat moss as the organic material, add ground limestone at the rate of 5 pounds per 100 square feet.

If you add raw sawdust that has not been composted or fortified with nitrogen (if it's been nitrogen fortified, it will say so on the bag), the amount of fertilizer will have to be increased slightly to take care of the bacteria that go to work on the sawdust. Without additional nitrogen, the bacteria will rob the soil of nitrogen while breaking down the sawdust.

For every 10 cubic feet of unfortified sawdust, add ½ pound of nitrogen. That means 10 pounds of 5-10-10 or 4 pounds of blood meal. And that means 18 pounds of 5-10-10 per 100 square feet of sawdust 2 inches thick.

The following table shows how much sawdust or similar organic material is needed to cover 100 square feet of that clayey or sandy soil to various depths.

Inches of Organic Material	To cover 100 Square Feet
6	2 cu. yds.
4	35 cu. ft.
3	1 cu. yd.
2	18 cu. ft.
1	9 cu. ft.
½	2 cu. ft..
¼	1 cu. ft.

1 cubic yard = 27 cubic feet

Shallow soils. Shallow topsoil, or no topsoil at all, is unfortunately a common problem. Many times, builders of new homes drastically alter the surface soil and leave a thin layer of topsoil over a fill layer of trash and subsoil.

If your problem area is not large, good quality topsoil can be hauled in to replenish what has been taken away. If the area is large, importing topsoils can be an expensive proposition. An alternative is to use the method described on page 44 for transforming subsoils into topsoils. It isn't an overnight process, but the results are worthwhile and long lasting.

If you are plagued with shallow soil and only want to garden a small area, your best bet is to confine your gardening to containers and raised beds, both of which can be filled with synthetic soil mixes (see page 40).

If you want to plant deep-rooted perennials or trees in a shallow soil, see page 82.

Poorly drained soils. Poorly drained soils are unproductive for most garden crops. The installation of tile drains is the most lasting and expensive method of treating this difficulty. In cases where the water comes primarily from adjoining higher land, an intercepting drain or ditch may be all that is necessary. Where drainage is impossible, or impossibly expensive to install, one must be content with growing only those plants that can tolerate "wet feet," or grow plants in raised beds (see page 42).

Saline soils. Salt-affected soils occur mostly in regions of arid or semiarid climates. They do not have the annual 30 to 40 inches of rain necessary to leach the salts through the soil. In most desert areas, the irrigation water itself may be high in salts. Fertilizers and manures add their share. Water that carries salts evaporates, and the salt accumulation builds up to a concentration injurious to plant growth.

A high degree of salinity greatly reduces the types of plants that can be grown. In most methods of dealing with salinity, the salts are leached away from the root zone where they do the most harm.

One such common method is the furrow system. It is used for growing vegetables in desert saline soils but will benefit other types of garden plants as well.

Where vegetables are planted, their relation to the furrow carrying the irrigation water determines the success or failure of the planting. The best possible location of a plant is where the water will move *through* the root zone, carrying the salts beyond it.

Water in a furrow will move radially downward or "sub" through the soil at each side of the furrow. Water moving through the soil carries the salts with it to the center of the bed if enough water is applied. Planting near the edge of the bed will avoid injury from salt accumulation. Do not plant on the crown or high point of a furrow.

With all types of irrigation—sprinklers, drip, ooze or flooding—water must be applied so that it drains through the soil.

The University of New Mexico recommends the furrow irrigation methods illustrated below. Each is designed to avoid the concentration of salts in the root zone.

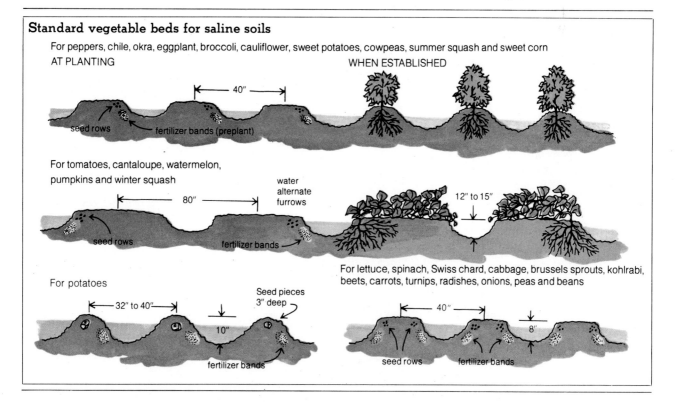

Standard vegetable beds for saline soils

For peppers, chile, okra, eggplant, broccoli, cauliflower, sweet potatoes, cowpeas, summer squash and sweet corn

AT PLANTING

WHEN ESTABLISHED

40"

seed rows — fertilizer bands (preplant)

For tomatoes, cantaloupe, watermelon, pumpkins and winter squash

80"

water alternate furrows

12" to 15"

seed rows — fertilizer bands

For lettuce, spinach, Swiss chard, cabbage, brussels sprouts, kohlrabi, beets, carrots, turnips, radishes, onions, peas and beans

For potatoes

32" to 40"

Seed pieces 3" deep

10"

fertilizer bands

40"

8"

seed rows — fertilizer bands

Synthetic Soils

For the small-space gardener— the gardener who concentrates on growing plants in pots, tubs, boxes or raised beds—nurseries and garden stores have "soilless mixes" and "synthetic soils" that offer many advantages over garden soil. Synthetic mixes are free of disease organisms, insects and weed seeds. They are lightweight —one-half the weight of regular garden soil when wet. Their light weight is an advantage when growing plants on rooftops or balconies.

Although the mixes are referred to as soilless mixes or synthetic soils, the word synthetic should not be translated as artificial. The ingredients are as natural as Mother Nature can make them.

Cornell and the University of California (U.C.) pioneered in formulating the soilless mixes for commercial plant growers. Based on their formulas, many mixes are available under several labels: Redi-Earth, Jiffy Mix, Metro Mix, Super Soil, Pro-Mix and many others. The basic difference between the two original mixes was the use of vermiculite in the Cornell mix and sand in the U.C. mix.

The basic ingredients

The organic fraction of the mix may be peat moss, redwood sawdust, wood shavings, bark of hardwoods, fir or pine bark, or a combination of any two of these.

The mineral fraction may be vermiculite, perlite, pumice, builder's sand or granite sand, or a combination of two or three. The most commonly used minerals are vermiculite, perlite and fine sand.

Vermiculite (Terralite) when mined resembles mica. Under heat treatment the mineral flakes expand with air spaces to 20 times their original thickness. Golden brown in color.

Perlite (sponge rock) when mined is a granitelike volcanic material that, when crushed and heat treated (1500°F to 2000°F, or 816°C to 1093°C), pops like popcorn and expands to 20 times its original volume. White in color.

The mix you buy may be half peat moss and half vermiculite, or half ground bark and half fine sand, or some other combination of the organic and mineral components. Although the ingredients in the mixes vary, the principles behind all mixes are the same: soilless mixes must provide (1) fast

drainage of water through the mix, (2) air in the mix after drainage, (3) moisture in the mix after drainage.

Most important in any container mix is the second item. The mix *must* retain air after drainage. Plant roots require air for growth and respiration.

In a heavy garden soil, the pore space between soil particles is small. When water is applied to the soil, it drives out air by filling these small spaces. In a container mix, there are small and large pores (micropores and macropores). When the mix is irrigated, water is retained in the micropores but quickly drains through the macropores, allowing air to follow. For an illustration of this action, see page 75.

The simpler the better

Gardeners who believe that every type of plant requires a special soil mix and like to work out complicated mixes of five or six ingredients find it difficult to accept the fact that a simple combination of peat moss and vermiculite (or perlite or fine sand) can be used with almost all types of plants, from cacti to tropicals.

This doesn't mean that the mix you buy shouldn't be tampered

More Mix Recipes

You may be going at container gardening in a big way, with large containers for shrubs and trees. Or are you planning to fill raised beds with your own mix? Before you try any of the formulas that follow, consider the advantages of buying the prepared commercial mixes, and consider your needs.

Few home gardeners need large quantities of a mix designed for seedlings and small pots. And, when growing seedlings or growing seed in pots, sterilization of the growing medium is all-important. When you need only a few cubic feet of container "soil," buying one of the commercial mixes is probably cheaper for you as well as easier.

In all these formulas, we have substituted 5-10-10 fertilizer for the combinations of superphosphate and calcium or potassium nitrate used in the original Cornell formula.

However, if you want to make your own, these are the components you would blend together to get about 1 yard of very lightweight mix for seedlings in pots:

> 9 cubic feet of peat moss
> 9 cubic feet of vermiculite
> 9 cubic feet of perlite
> 5 pounds of 5-10-10 fertilizer
> 5 pounds of ground limestone

For a slightly heavier mix for seedlings in pots:

> 14 cubic feet of peat moss
> 7 cubic feet of fine sand
> 7 cubic feet of perlite
> 5 pounds of 5-10-10 fertilizer
> 8 pounds of ground limestone

A mix recommended for indoor foliage plants goes like this:

> 14 cubic feet of peat moss
> 7 cubic feet of vermiculite
> 7 cubic feet of perlite
> 5 pounds of 5-10-10 fertilizer
> 1 pound of iron sulfate
> 8 pounds of ground limestone

The proportions for a mix for shrubs and trees are:

> 18 cubic feet of ground bark or nitrogen-stabilized sawdust
> 9 cubic feet of fine sand

> **or**

> 9 cubic feet of peat moss
> 9 cubic feet of ground bark
> 9 cubic feet of fine sand

Add to either of the above formulas:

> 5 pounds of 5-10-10 fertilizer
> 7 pounds of ground limestone
> 1 pound of iron sulfate

with. If the mix is so lightweight that the container will tip over in a slight wind, add sand. Many gardeners add garden topsoil to the mix when planting shrubs or trees in containers. But when soil is added, all the advantages of a sterilized mix are lost. If you are using the soilless mix for growing tomatoes in containers to avoid soilborne tomato diseases, you should not add any garden soil at all.

The soilless mixes are ready to use as they are. All the nutrients needed for initial plant growth are included in the mix. Bring home a bag—2 cubic feet—and you have enough mix for 20 to 22 one-gallon containers, or 35 to 40 six-inch pots. You would need 4 cubic feet of mix to fill a planter box 48 by 18 by 8 inches deep.

A basic mix
For one reason or another, you want to make your own mix. Here's how to go about it.

If your containers receive frequent spring and fall rains, use perlite rather than vermiculite. If your mix is to be used in shrub and tree containers, use a combination of 1/3 sand and 2/3 ground bark or peat moss.

The mixing process is the same for all mixes. To make about 1 cubic yard of mix, take:

14 cubic feet of peat moss—or nitrogen-stabilized fir or pine bark—and the same amount of vermiculite or perlite
or
18 cubic feet of ground bark and 9 cubic feet of fine sand
or
14 cubic feet of peat moss and 7 cubic feet of vermiculite and 7 cubic feet of perlite.

Dump the ingredients in a pile and roughly mix them. Dampen the mix as you go. Dry peat moss is far easier to wet with warm water than with cold.

After dampening the mix, spread these fertilizer elements over it:

5 pounds of ground limestone and 5 pounds of a 5-10-10 fertilizer that includes trace elements—the micronutrients described on page 50.

Mix by shoveling the ingredients with a scoop shovel into a cone shaped pile, letting each shovelful dribble down the cone. To get a thoroughly mixed product, rebuild the cone three to five times (see illustration). The only way we know to get a more even

mix is with a mechanical mixer.

If a smaller quantity will take care of your needs, cut down on all the ingredients in proportion.

If the mix is not to be used soon after mixing, store in plastic bags or plastic garbage cans.

Note: The pile will shrink 15 to 20 percent in mixing because of the loss of air space. One cubic yard equals 27 cubic feet or 22 bushels. One full yard of mix, however, requires an additional 5 cubic feet or 4 bushels—which means, in order to obtain a full cubic yard of mix, use a total of 26 bushels or 32 cubic feet of raw materials.

Use of waste products
Among the organic ingredients listed in the contents of synthetic mixes are products that were once classed as waste—fir bark, pine bark, redwood sawdust. Such commercially available materials have been thoroughly tested for toxicity, pH reaction, and uniformity. Other waste products can be used, and more and more such products will become available as less and less green material is burned or buried. Take a look in want ads and bulletin boards for locally available materials.

Making your own soil mix

Store bought soil mixes contain these ingredients . . .

You can make your own soil mix by using one of the formulas in the text and mixing it very thoroughly. By "very thoroughly" we mean that it must be mixed so each portion, even a 2" potful, has the proper portions of each ingredient. To mix it well follow these steps:
1. Pour the dampened peat moss and perlite or vermiculite in a rough pile. Sprinkle the fertilizer and lime on top.

2. Shoveling from the first pile, make a cone-shaped pile by pouring each shovelful directly on top so ingredients dribble down the sides.
3. Shovel from the second pile and repeat the cone-shaped pile building and dribbling.
4. Do it again. Make a third cone-shaped pile. It's then ready to use.

Raised Beds

The raised bed concept is one we have recommended for many years in various Ortho Books. The idea is certainly not a new one. The principle of planting above the land level has been applied throughout gardening history. We become more convinced of the merits of raised beds with the passing of each gardening season.

A raised bed establishes a structure in which the gardener can effectively meet a plant's basic requirements. Soil conditioning can be concentrated within it, with good results.

There are many variations of the raised bed theme but they all have these virtues:

Speeds up spring planting. In a wet, cool spring the soil in the raised bed will warm up and be ready for planting weeks before regular garden soils can be planted.

Never too much rain. With soil raised above ground level, drainage away from the bed is possible. Unless the soil around the bed is flooded, the raised bed will never be waterlogged.

No-kneel gardens. When made with a wide cap, the raised bed doubles as a bench, making it possible to sit while you weed. Cultivating can be done with a trowel rather than a hoe.

Always neater. As a clean and neat structure, the bed makes the gardener want to keep the planting clean and neat. Weeds are more distracting in a raised bed than in an equal amount of space hidden in a corner of the garden.

Gives order to the garden. The color of flowers and vegetables comes and goes with the seasons; the raised bed can be an attractive element in the garden in spring, summer, fall and winter.

Pleases the specialists. Herb gardeners and collectors of miniature bulbs, cacti or succulents appreciate the restraint and the comfortable closeness of the raised bed.

Protects plants. Outdoor furniture and wheeled toys can bump up against the sides of raised beds

No matter what the size, when a raised bed is filled with a good soil, the results are the same—success for the gardener.

without injuring the plants.

Gophers and moles can be excluded from raised bed plantings by enclosing the bottom of the bed with close-meshed galvanized screen before the bed is filled with soil. Protection from birds can be managed with wire or nylon netting. The wood frame of the raised bed lets you add other protective devices.

Wheelchair gardens. Raised beds can be built to wheelchair height and make gardening available to all who find it satisfying.

Air in the soil. Even without special conditioning, soil held above ground level will provide better drainage than the soil around it. With the addition of organic matter, the soil can be tailored to special plant requirements. If you want to grow blueberries in an area with alkaline soil, fill a raised bed with acid soil.

There is no chance for compaction of soil in a raised bed. There is no need to walk on the soil and no need for machinery.

Continuous water supply. Drip irrigation can be managed more easily in a raised bed than in a normal garden situation. A mulch of plastic film (easily held in place) will conserve moisture and make its delivery to the plants more uniform.

Continuous nutrient supply. Regardless of the method, fertilizing can be carried out more efficiently in raised beds. The area to be covered is exactly known. For instance, you may have two beds, each 4 feet wide and 12 feet long. The two areas total 96 square feet. When the fertilizer instructions are stated in pounds per 100 square feet, it's easy to be on target.

The formal raised bed

4 × 4 post every 6 feet

For just a few inches of depth, construction can be as simple as this . . .

cap

2 × 6

Deeper raised beds with a cap or seat cap have additional landscape functions.

Seat cap of 2 × 4s

Railroad ties make ideal raised beds. They can be used singly or up to 3 deep.

Railroad ties

Rock walls are less stiff and harsh than wooden raised beds—and you can plant in the cracks.

Slope at least 1 inch per each foot of height

Stones or broken concrete

Short lengths of logs, poles or grapestakes driven into the soil

Good quality topsoil may be too expensive to import for an entire garden plot, but when confined to raised beds, its use may be well justified. These beds were filled with topsoil excavated from another part of the yard and mixed with organic soil amendments to create a first-class vegetable garden.

Commercial Topsoils

Some garden supply stores and large nurseries sell topsoil by the cubic yard, and in some areas there are companies that will deliver loads of topsoil to your home. Buying topsoil in this manner has both advantages and disadvantages, depending on its quality and intended use.

First off, the gardener should be aware that "topsoil" as a substance sold to consumers has no strict or legal definition, as do fertilizers. Topsoils can be many things: good river loam, rocky subsoil of low fertility, or a mixture of many types of soils.

As a gardener you should try to find out, as best you can, the origin and nature of the topsoil you are buying—before you buy it. It should be free of noxious weed seeds, and free of disease. You have to take the word of the seller concerning weed seeds and disease, because there is no real way to tell if they are present until after you've had the soil in your garden for a while.

Furthermore, if you are intending to supplement poor or nonexistent topsoil in your garden, importing topsoil can become an expensive solution if the area to be improved is large. Imported

topsoils are most judiciously used in confined areas, such as garden plots or raised beds, and ideally should be mixed with organic soil amendments—peat moss, compost, well-rotted manure, or fortified sawdust—and vermiculite or perlite (see Synthetic Soils, page 40).

In its *Handbook on Soils*, the Brooklyn Botanic Garden asks the question:

"Why haul in topsoil for lawn or garden?" and has this to say:

"In nature, subsoil is being constantly, though slowly, converted into topsoil. Experiments have shown that this conversion can be greatly speeded up by man. At the Ohio Agricultural Experiment Station, land from which the topsoil had been completely stripped has been restored to productivity. The subsoil was treated with lime, manure, and fertilizer, and planted to various rotations of crops. Green manures [see page 56], especially alfalfa, were freely used to aid the conversion.

"Home gardeners may be interested in a recent subsoil-to-topsoil conversion that was carried out at the Brooklyn Botanic Garden. The subsoil area (hardpan) to be planted in lawn was first plowed in mid-August. Sever-

al loads of well-rotted manure were spread over the plowed ground—about 3 to 4 times as much as would be used for ordinary manuring. Sand, ground limestone, and 5-10-5 [fertilizer] were liberally applied, and the whole area well worked over with a rotary hoe. After being allowed to settle, the area was graded and seeded with Merion bluegrass. A vigorous lawn became established by June of the following season. Weeds have been a minor problem, no worse than in any lawn with which we have had experience. The same technique has been successfully employed for preparation of a vegetable garden site on subsoil. One final word of caution: add enough coarse sand to insure soil aeration and good drainage.

"By way of explanation: subsoil is often as rich as the overlying topsoil in all mineral nutrients except nitrogen and sometimes phosphorus and potash. It is lacking in organic material, and usually has a poor structure. These are the factors which must be dealt with in remaking subsoil. Nitrogen fertilizers must be added, and liming may be needed if the subsoil is too acid. Organic matter (in the form of compost, manure, etc.) is one of the essentials."

Tilling

Tillers have come a long way since the 1700s when Jethro Tull invented the first horse-pulled cultivator he called a "horse-hoe." Today there is a wide range of rototiller models, and personal preference as much as intended use seems to dictate the choice.

There are small, electrically powered cultivators which some gardeners call "chicken scratchers." There are medium and large gasoline-powered rototillers with the tillers in the rear, and large rototillers with the tillers in the front of the machine. And there are all sizes of multipurpose tractor models.

You'll know which type is best for you, but a few guidelines can be observed. If you are a serious gardener and intend to use a rototiller frequently, it's a good idea to buy the largest model you can afford. Smaller models will fill the bill for gardeners who use a rototiller only occasionally and for light jobs. Remember, the larger the rototiller, the less and easier the work. And check the size of the engine as well as the size of the tillers—the size of the tillers regulates the depth you can till.

If you're in the market for a large handheld rototiller, test gardeners we know favor the models with the tillers in the front, which have the effect of pulling the machine through the soil and making the operation smoother.

Rototillers are used for two general operations: mixing soil amendments and fertilizers into garden soil, and preparing soil to make it into an acceptable bed for vegetable, grass or other seed.

When you rototill amendments and fertilizers into the soil, the intent is to do a thorough job, and several pass-throughs may be necessary. But when you're preparing a seedbed, it's possible to overdo a good thing. If your garden area is several seasons old and you've added organic matter each year, the soil probably has a good structure that promotes healthy root growth and proper air and water retention. Over-rototilling and raking to the point where the soil is in very fine

particles destroys this structure temporarily, and with the first application of water, you'll have a big mud pie. When the soil dries out after watering, the seeds will be imprisoned by a tight crust on the surface of the soil.

Remember, too, that you can do serious damage to the soil structure by rototilling when the soil is too wet. When you are able to crumble the soil apart with your fingers, instead of getting a sticky mess, the soil is dry enough to till.

A large rototiller, with the tines in the rear, makes a big job easier and smoother.

Tillers come in many sizes and models: tines in front or at rear; small models in gas or electric versions; large, multipurpose tractor models.

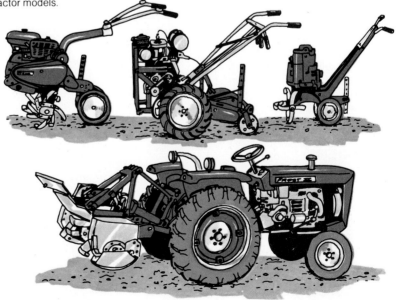

Composting

Garden waste material can be converted in many ways into a black, fragrant, crumbly, partially decomposed organic residue called compost.

In all composting your objective is to arrange organic waste material in such a way that soil bacteria and fungi can thrive and multiply as they break it down. The bacteria are the converters of the raw material and they must have a workable environment. They need moisture, air and food.

Basic method

Make the compost with a mixture of green and dry materials. Grass clippings, green weeds, lettuce leaves, pea vines and other succulent materials contain sugar and proteins that are excellent food for the bacteria. They are decomposed rapidly. Sawdust, dry leaves, small twigs and prunings contain very little nitrogen and decompose very slowly when composted alone. A mixture of the green and the dry is what you want.

Gardeners have found that the best way to build a compost pile is to put a layer of mixed fertilizer, manure and garden soil between each layer of waste material.

You start the pile by spreading a layer of the organic refuse about 6 to 8 inches deep. Spread over this layer the mixture of manure, garden soil and fertilizer. Both manure and a commercial fertilizer should be used to give the bacteria the mineral nutrients they need. The greater the amount of fertilizer, the richer the compost will be. A good average amount in each layer is 2 cupfuls of ammonium sulfate or blood meal per square foot. Use more with dry waste material, less with green material.

Wet down the fertilizer layer just enough to carry the chemicals through the layer; don't wash them out with heavy watering.

In areas where the soil is on the acid side, adding a cupful of ground limestone, crushed oyster shell or dolomite lime to each layer will give you a less acid product.

This compost bin was constructed three years ago in one of our test gardens. It has proved to be an excellent design, and the finished product an important part of our gardening habits. What comes from the soil is returned to the soil.

Add another layer of vegetable matter, spread the soil-manure-chemical layer over it and wet it down. Repeat the layering process until you run out of material or the pile is 4 to 5 feet high.

Keep the pile as wet as a squeezed-out sponge. In a dry, warm climate, it may need water every 4 to 5 days.

The size of the woody material will affect the rate of decomposition. If dry leaves go into the pile as they are raked up, decomposition will be much slower than if the leaves are shredded.

Under normal conditions the pile should be turned 2 to 3 weeks after you start it, then about every 5 weeks. It should be ready to use in 3 months.

Grass clippings. If you produce grass clippings in large quantities, you must mix them thoroughly into the composting material to avoid odor and fly problems. A good load of grass clippings will make a soggy mass, and putrify instead of decaying normally. Flies seem to regard a mass of clippings as an egg incubator. To avoid this problem, spread a layer of soil or old compost over the top of the pile after mixing the grass into the compost.

Fast, high-heat method

You can shorten the ripening time for a compost to a few weeks if all the refuse material is put through a shredder before building the pile. The smaller pieces decompose faster since more sur-

face is exposed to decay bacteria. Shredding also makes a fluffier mixture, allowing more efficient air and water penetration. If renting or buying a shredder is not in your program, shred all large leaves with a rotary mower.

If the pile is built when the weather is warm, you'll see heat waves rising above it in 24 to 30 hours. Turn the pile to mix the material and follow up with a thorough watering. It will heat up again, and in a few days be hot enough to require turning again. Each time you turn it, move outer materials toward the center where heat and moisture encourage decomposition.

One distinct advantage to this fast, high-heat method of composting is the destruction of most of the weed seeds.

The compost is ready for use when it has cooled, has a dark and rich color, is crumbly and has that good earth fragrance.

It pays to divide your composting area into three piles or compartments. The first compartment is for the daily collection of the organic waste—vegetable harvest refuse, vegetable peelings from the kitchen, coffee grounds, egg shells, shredded paper, small prunings, wood ashes, and weeds green or dry. The next compartment is for the working compost to which no additions are being made but frequent turning is the rule. The third compartment is for the finished or nearly finished product.

Building a Bin

This is the Rolls Royce of compost bins. After three years of constant use, its design has been well proven.

The bin will hold generous amounts of compost and is designed to provide the air circulation so important for proper decomposition. View the bin as four dividers that are held sturdily by the boards across the back and by the pipe reinforcement at the front.

All the materials—except the filler strips and the removable boards—can be precut to the lengths called out in the materials list. Start construction by joining parts B and C. Note the 2 by 4s of the inside dividers are centered on the 2 by 6s; those on the end dividers are attached along an edge.

Join these subassemblies by nailing on all of the boards, part D. Remember to leave the 1-inch space at the front (see detail in drawing). After you add the filler strips, you will have a groove for the removable boards to slide in. The last step on the dividers before you attach part A is to nail on part E to cover the opening left by the two bottom boards.

Prepare the bin area, preferably in a sunny location, by leveling and tamping the ground. Space the dividers to provide the overall length you decide on and then add the three back boards, part G.

When driving the pipes, hold them snugly against the front surface of the dividers. Keep them centered so they will stay vertical. Use a sledge hammer to do the job (or a special pipe driver), but don't attempt to swing like a railroad worker. Settle for driving the pipe as far in as you can. If the ground is too hard for a full 3-foot penetration, then use a hacksaw to cut the top ends and use a file to remove the burrs. Add the pipe clamps, using large, panhead, sheet-metal screws instead of conventional wood screws; they will hold better.

Apply any chemically inactive finish material, such as a water seal, before you staple the wire fabric in place.

Materials needed

A = four 5-foot lengths of 2 by 6
B = eight 34½-inch lengths of 2 by 6
C = eight 34½-inch lengths of 2 by 4
D = eighteen 54½-inch lengths of 1 by 6 — use boards or cut from exterior-grade plywood
E = two 47½-inch lengths of 1 by 3
F = stock length of 1 by 2 — cut to suit
G = three 9-foot lengths of 2 by 6
H = optional number of 1 by 6 boards or exterior-grade plywood — cut lengths to suit
Four 6-foot lengths of ¾-inch galvanized pipe 12 pipe straps with screws
About 45 feet of yard-wide wire fabric

All Mat. = Const. Grade Heart Redwood, Stock Widths

Line inside of bins with ½" × ½" or 1" × 1" galvanized 16 or 14 gauge welded wire fabric (36" high). Attach with galvanized fence staples.

Treat bottom 2 × 6s with wood preservatives such as "Copper Green" or "Cuprinol."

Removable 1x boards

1x filler strips

Pipe driven into ground for support

Galvanized pipe at each post. Secure with pipe clamps and screws.

1x covers

1 × 6

3'

E

G

2 × 6

3'

C

A

D

2 × 6

B

2 × 4

2 × 6

5'

3'

9'

3'

1"

Fertilizers

Satisfying a plant's need for the essential nutrients
can be handled in many ways. The information
in this chapter will help you match the right fertilizer
with the right plant, using the most effective method.

I f you are reading this book
from front to back, you already know that garden soils
are a combination of organic and
mineral components. There are
nutrients in both of these components, and two processes make
the nutrients available for use by
the plant: (1) living soil organisms
—often referred to as beneficial
bacteria—break down and release the nutrients found in the
organic matter; (2) the natural
process of degradation—the
effects of sun, wind and freezing
rain—make the *mineral elements* available.

Knowing this, the next logical
question is usually, "Why, if there
are nutrients already in the soil, is
it necessary to add fertilizers?"

The answer is a simple one:
Although the amount of nutrients
in most soils is relatively high in
comparison to a plant's requirements, much of this potential
supply is unfortunately in a form
plants cannot use, or the nutrients
are not supplied fast enough to
produce satisfactory plant growth.
Farmers and gardeners alike turn
to fertilizers to make up for this
deficiency. Thus, fertilizers play a
considerable part in keeping
plants at the peak of their
performance.

All fertilizers, whether natural,
organic or synthesized, contain
some or all of the nutrient elements essential for plant growth.
In whatever amounts they are
present, these elements are
what make a fertilizer a fertilizer.

The Essential Plant Nutrients

There are currently more than
100 known chemical elements.
Of these, there are only 16 that
have definitely been determined
to be essential for plant growth
and another one that recent research suggests may be essential.
These elements are considered
essential because without any one
of them, plant growth will not
occur even if the other elements
are present in their required
amounts.

The realization that these elements are essential has had a pro-
found effect on our knowledge of
plant nutrition. For centuries farmers and gardeners have known
that the addition of certain substances (manure, ashes, blood
meal) had a positive effect on

The value of fertilizers has been well known throughout gardening history and is.dramati-
cally illustrated in this photograph. These two tomato plants were started at the same time.
The plant on the left received regular fertilizer applications; the one on the right did not.
It is particularly important to provide short-season annual crops, such as vegetables, with
the nutrients they need. Any check in nutrient availability will affect growth and production.

Some plants have special nutrient needs. Citrus plants frequently suffer from chlorosis and should be fed with a formulation containing additional amounts of iron and zinc.

plant growth, but even as recently as 1800 it was not known which elements used by plants were indispensable. As scientific methods become even more refined, it may be that we will discover even more "essential" elements.

The following is a list of the 16 elements known now to be essential for plant growth. The first three are derived primarily from the atmosphere and water.

Carbon (C)
Hydrogen (H)
Oxygen (O)

Macronutrients:
Nitrogen (N)
Phosphorus (P)
Potassium (K)

Secondary nutrients:
Calcium (Ca)
Magnesium (Mg)
Sulfur (S)

Micronutrients:
Boron (B)
Chlorine (Cl)
Copper (Cu)
Iron (Fe)
Manganese (Mn)
Molybdenum (Mo)
Zinc (Zn)

One further element—cobalt—is thought to be essential for specific groups of plants.

Carbon, hydrogen and oxygen are supplied primarily by air and water. The other elements are absorbed by plant roots from the surrounding soil. These 13 elements are of primary importance to the farmer and gardener. They are most often supplied by the soil, and/or by the application of fertilizers.

The essential elements are divided into three categories: macronutrients, secondary nutrients and micronutrients. This system of classification is based on the relative amounts of the three groups of elements that are normally found in plants, and does *not* imply relative importance: they are all essential.

Macronutrients

The macronutrients—nitrogen, phosphorus and potassium—are considered the three primary mineral elements necessary for plant growth. You may see them referred to as N, P and K, their respective chemical symbols. But for most gardeners, nitrogen, phosphate and potash are the

three numbers on a fertilizer's label: the fertilizer's analysis. A fertilizer is said to be "complete" when it contains a percentage of each, even though the macronutrients are only 3 out of the essential mineral elements provided by fertilizer.

While it is true that the essential elements are all important, most home gardeners will get by handily with a working knowledge of the three macronutrients: nitrogen, phosphorus and potassium. Because of their special importance, we have devoted a page to each of the macronutrients (pages 51, 53 and 55). We strongly recommend reading these pages. The information will help you to make a more confident, educated choice of fertilizer when at a nursery or garden store.

Secondary nutrients

The three secondary nutrients—calcium, magnesium and sulfur—are the "in-betweens" of the essential plant nutrients. They are present in some fertilizer formulations, and not in others. Generally speaking, though, they are available in most soils in adequate amounts, or tag along as part of fertilizers, soil amendments or conditioners such as lime and gypsum.

Calcium and magnesium. In areas of the country where lime is applied to the soil to correct acid conditions (usually in areas of substantial rainfall), the plant may receive adequate amounts of calcium and, if you use dolomitic limestone, magnesium as a part of the lime. Lime can be added to the soil in several forms: agricultural lime, dolomite, marl and others.

In areas where the soil is neutral to alkaline, there is normally enough calcium and magnesium naturally available in the soil to supply a plant's needs. In some cases there may be a magnesium deficiency. Symptoms of a magnesium deficiency include chlorosis (yellowing) of older leaves; upturned curling of leaf margins; and marginal yellowing with green "Christmas tree" shape in the center of the leaf. Epsom salts (magnesium sulfate) can be added to supply magnesium.

Nitrogen (N)

It is for good reason that nitrogen is listed as the first of the primary nutrients needed for normal plant growth. Compared with the other essential nutrients, nitrogen is the one that is usually absorbed by plants from the soil in the greatest quantity. The effects of optimum levels of nitrogen are marked; similarly, a deficiency of nitrogen has pronounced physiological effects.

Nitrogen, in adequate supply, is necessary for rapid growth, and imparts to leaves and stems a characteristically deep green, healthy color. The most apparent function of nitrogen is the encouragement of aboveground vegetative growth.

Nitrogen is present in all young, tender parts of plant tissues—tips of shoots, buds and opening leaves—chiefly as protein. As new cells form, much of this protein may move from the older cells (the mature leaves) to the newer ones. If the available nitrogen begins to fall short of the plant's needs, what nitrogen is available is used by the new shoots at the expense of the older leaves.

This phenomenon is the cause of the characteristic general yellowing of mature leaves in nitrogen-deficient plants.

Where does it come from?

Nitrogen enters plants as NO_3^- (nitrate) or, less frequently, as NH_3 (ammonia). All the nitrogen that is available for a plant's use originates from the atmosphere, organic matter in the soil—and a little from the mineral fraction—and from fertilizers.

The atmosphere is 78 percent nitrogen by volume. At sea level there are approximately 34,500 tons of nitrogen present in the atmosphere over one acre of land. This nitrogen is present as inert N_2 gas, a form that, in fact, resists reacting with other elements. The atmospheric nitrogen that does make its way to a plant's root zone is oxidized nitrogen, a product of lightning storms and other ionizing phenomena in the upper atmosphere, carried to the soil via rainfall. The process of converting N_2 into a form plants can use is called *nitrogen fixation.* Certain microorganisms present in the soil are also responsible for a conversion of some of the N_2 into usable forms.

The organic matter that is natural in the soil or has been added by the gardener also contains nitrogen. But once again it is present in a form—a complex protein—that cannot be used by plants, except as it is made available by various microorganisms. This process of converting the nitrogen in organic matter into a usable form is called *mineralization* or *ammonification.* The beneficial microorganisms decompose organic matter to obtain a supply of energy for their own growth. In the process, they liberate ammonia, some of which they use themselves. But the rest is set free as a by-product and may be subsequently used by the plant. Most soil nitrogen is contained in organic matter, at any given time. Soil microorganisms mineralize a small portion of that total each year. These microorganisms are not active during periods of low soil temperatures. Microbial activity becomes significant at about 45° to 50°F and the rate doubles for each rise of 18°F in temperature (assuming adequate moisture and favorable soil environment).

Fertilizers. The amount of nitrogen converted from the atmosphere and from organic matter may be inadequate compared with the needs of most plants. That's why we add fertilizers. These can be broken down into two general groups: organic and inorganic. Representative examples each group and how the gardener should handle them are described on pages 64 to 65.

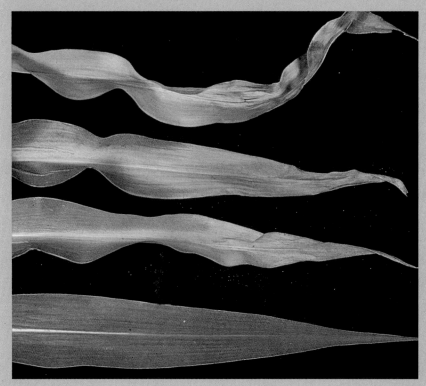

Nitrogen deficiencies frequently show up as a yellowing of the mature leaves of the plant, and a general slowing in the growth rate. Because nitrogen has a dramatic effect on the growth of plants, it should be applied only when plants are growing, not when they are dormant.

Chlorosis is defined as the lack of green color in a leaf. It is frequently caused by a lack of iron in the plant. Many times the whole leaf will turn yellowish, except for the veins, which stay green, resembling a Christmas tree pattern.

Sulfur. This element is just as essential as nitrogen in the making of new protoplasm for plant cells, but its deficiency in the soil is not so prevalent. Moreover, sulfur naturally found in the soil is in organic matter. Upon decomposition, the sulfur—like nitrogen—is released for the plants to use. In addition to receiving sulfur from the soil, plants also receive it from the atmosphere in industrial areas, in the form of sulfur dioxide (SO_2). But if the concentration of SO_2 is too high, it will kill plant tissue.

Micronutrients

Although the amounts of the micronutrients—boron, iron, manganese, copper, zinc, molybdenum and chlorine—a plant needs are relatively small, they are just as essential for plant growth as the larger amounts of macronutrients and secondary nutrients.

As a rule, home gardeners add specific micronutrients to the soil only when deficiency symptoms occur on the plant in the garden. Many commercial fertilizers contain micronutrients as part of the formulation. Along with listing the percentages of the three macronutrients, some manufacturers also list the micronutrients and

their percentages. On the other hand, just because there are no micronutrients listed on the label, it doesn't necessarily mean there are none in the formulation. The law requires that the manufacturer guarantee the analysis claimed on the label. Because the micronutrients are in such small quantities, it can be so difficult to substantiate the claim that the manufacturer just does not claim them. All of this is of little concern

to most gardeners because the absence of a particular micronutrient is seldom a problem in most home garden soils.

Chelates

On the labels of some specialty fertilizers, you will see the word "chelate" or "contains chelated iron." Chelating agents are synthetic organic substances that have the property of maintaining copper, manganese, zinc and iron in a nonionized, water-soluble form so that these micronutrients may be readily absorbed by plants.

Chelates are used to correct chlorosis in plants. Chlorosis is the lack of green color in a leaf. It may be caused by nutritional deficiency, disease or toxins. It is frequently caused by the lack of iron in the plant. In severe cases the entire leaf, except the veins, turns yellow. Often there is enough iron in the soil, but it's locked in, or fixed into insoluble compounds that are unavailable to the plant. When a chelating agent with the micronutrient is added, the nutrient element is made available to the plant.

Organic fertilizers

Almost all the organic fertilizers share certain advantages and disadvantages. Usually they act more slowly than synthetic fertilizers, making it more difficult to

Rock phosphate is mined in many areas of the United States. It's phosphorus content ranges from 27 to 41 percent. Superphosphate, a common form of phosphorus fertilizer, is rock phosphate treated with sulfuric acid to make it more soluble.

Phosphorus (P)

Phosphorus, the second of the three macronutrients, is essential in all phases of plant growth, but is particularly associated with early maturity of crops (most notably the cereal crops), the formation of seeds and fruit, and increased root growth. Increased disease-resistance is another reported benefit when a plant is adequately supplied with phosphorus.

If the supply of phosphorus is too low to meet the plant's needs, the existing phosphorus will move from the older tissues to the younger tissues. Therefore, the usual visible signs of a lack of phosphorus appear first in the lower leaves, which are the older ones. The symptoms may be a lack of chlorophyll, a deepening of the green color, or a reddish color in the leaves. In an average garden soil, most of the total phosphorus supply is tied up in a chemical form that is not usable by the crop in a single growing season.

As organic matter mineral-izes, some phosphorus is released and some is dissolved from soil minerals and is made available to plants. This rate of release is very limited, however —producing only about 1 ppm at any one time. Phosphorus usually enters plants as $H_2PO_4^-$, that is, phosphate.

If phosphorus were more like nitrogen, gardeners could easily make up for the unavailable phosphorus by adding more in the form of fertilizer. But here's what happens: when a fertilizer containing phosphorus is applied to the soil surface, some of the phosphorus is fixed at the place where it is added—it doesn't move to the roots where it can be utilized—and some is fixed rapidly into a form that is, again, unavailable to plants. Only about 10 to 20 percent of the applied phosphorus is used by the plant within the year it is applied. Another phenomenon of phosphorus is that it does not move very far within the soil—approximately one inch from its original placement, unless physically moved by cultivation.

What can you do?

Gardeners can take several measures to make sure that plants are getting an adequate amount of phosphorus:

(1) Keep soil pH at levels between 6.0 and 7.0 (see *Soil pH,* page 26). Acid soils will fix phosphorus to a greater extent than neutral or slightly alkaline soils of the same texture.

(2) Use organic matter such as manure and crop residues ("green manure"). Soil microorganisms in the organic matter decompose the phosphorus, use it for a while and then release it in a form usable by plants.

(3) Because the movement of phosphorus is so limited within the soil, gardeners and farmers often apply phosphorus in "bands" below soil level, near the root zone.

(4) When planting trees and shrubs, you can use a method similar to banding. The roots will have a better chance at getting at the phosphorus if you mix a phosphorus fertilizer or a complete-formulation fertilizer with the soil you take from the hole (the backfill) and put that soil back in the root zone.

(5) Research has indicated that the availability of soil phosphorus is also affected by the available moisture supply. Thus, good watering practices will help maximize the available phosphorus.

One last note concerning phosphorus: Phosphorus availability is lowest in cool weather, so the addition is especially important in early spring plantings.

Phosphorus deficiencies are often difficult to detect because much of the effect of phosphorus is only apparent underground, in the root system of the plant. In corn, however, phosphorus deficiencies frequently show up as a reddish color in the leaves.

Spring-flowering bulbs, such as tulips, make good use of the slow-release quality of the phosphorus in bone meal. It can be added to the planting hole when the bulbs are planted in the fall.

over-fertilize. But those that have a low percentage of nitrogen are bulkier and heavier to handle because they have to be applied in much greater quantities. More important is the fact that they release the fertilizing elements somewhat unpredictably, when the soil is warm enough.

Bone meal. Bone meal decomposes slowly and hence it releases phosphate slowly. It is a good choice as a fertilizer for bulbs that don't sprout until several months after they are planted. It is a mild fertilizer which may be dug into the loose dirt at the bottom of the hole where a bulb is planted. Another advantage of bone meal is its alkaline chemistry. It helps neutralize the acidity of peat-based potting mixes, and makes a good additive for alkaline-loving plants such as cacti and succulents.

Cottonseed meal. A by-product of cotton manufacturing. As a fertilizer it is somewhat acid in reaction. Formulas vary slightly, but generally contain 7 percent nitrogen, 3 percent phosphorus, and 2 percent potash. Cottonseed meal is more readily available to plants in warm soils, but there is little danger of over-fertilizing. For general garden use apply 2-5 pounds per 1000 square feet. Used frequently for fertilizing acid-loving plants such as azaleas, camellias, and rhododendrons.

Blood meal. This is dried, powdered blood from cattle slaughterhouses. It is a rich source of nitrogen—so rich, in fact, that it may do harm if used in excess. Be careful not to exceed the recommended amount suggested on the label. In addition to nitrogen, blood meal supplies certain of the essential trace elements, including iron.

Fish emulsion. This well-rounded fertilizer is a partially decomposed blend of finely pulverized fish. No matter how little is used, the odor is intense but it dissipates within a day or two. Fish emulsion is high in nitrogen, and is a source of several trace elements. In the late

spring, when garden plants have sprouted, an application of fish emulsion followed by a deep watering will boost their early growth spurt. Contrary to popular belief, too strong a solution of fish emulsion can cause plants to "burn," particularly those in containers.

Manures. Commonly available manures include horse, cow, pig, chicken, and sheep products. The actual nutrient content varies widely: the highest concentration of nutrients is when manures are fresh and as it is aged, leached, or composted, nutrient content is reduced.

Even though fresh manures have the highest amount of nutrients, most gardeners prefer to use composted forms of manure to ensure a lesser amount of salts, thereby reducing the chance of burning plants. Fresh manure should not be used where it will come into contact with tender roots.

The chart on page 58 compares the nutrient content of several manures with some standard synthetic fertilizer formulations.

As you can see, compared to synthetic fertilizer formulations, manures contain relatively low concentrations of actual nutrients, but they perform other important functions which the synthetic formulations do not. Among them are: increasing the organic content of the soil; improving the phys-

ical structure of the soil; increasing the bacterial and fungal activity, particularly the mycorrhiza fungus, which alone makes other nutrients more available to plants.

Typical rates of manure applications vary from a moderate 70 pounds per 1000 square feet, to as much as one ton per 1000 square feet.

Seaweed extract. From the first level in the marine food chain, seaweed is another excellent source of trace metals. Moreover, it contains growth hormones that some horticulturists believe are active for the fertilized plants. Its relative lack of odor is an obvious advantage over fish emulsion. But the high cost is an equally obvious disadvantage. Today, seaweed extract is most commonly used for house plants. If current experimentation in the cultivation of kelp and other seaweeds is successful, it may become an economical fertilizer for the garden.

Sewage sludge is a recycled product of municipal sewage treatment plants. Two forms are commonly available: activated and composted. Activated sludge has higher concentrations of nutrients (approximately 6-3-5) than composted sludge, and is usually sold in a dry, granular form for use as a general purpose, longlasting, non-burning fertilizer.

Composted sludge is used

Potassium (K)

The third major element supplied in the fertilizer bag or bottle is potassium. Potassium —potash—is essential for the growth of plants, and plants take large amounts of it from the soil.

You will often see potassium referred to as "potash." The word potash goes back to colonial days when wood and other organic materials were burned in pots for the manufacture of soap. The ashes were rinsed with water; this rinse water was collected and allowed to evaporate. The residue was largely potassium salts. Today, potassium is mined in a similar manner to rock phosphate.

Potassium passes through the membranes of root hairs as the simple ion, K+.

The total potassium content of U.S. soils generally increases from east to west—that is, it increases in the direction of less severe soil weathering. The potassium content tends to increase from south to north in the eastern half of the country.

It is not known exactly what role potassium performs in the living processes of a plant cell, but there is some evidence that it acts in enzymatic processes, especially the transformations among different kinds of sugars. It is known, however, that potassium functions within the plant in a number of specialized ways. This nutrient increases the resistance of some plants to disease and it aids in the formation of oils in oil-bearing seeds. It improves the rigidity of stalks, and helps plants overcome the effects of adverse weather or soil conditions. In a general way, potassium contributes to the overall vigor of plants. Under normal growing conditions with adequate nutrient supplies, many plants use as much potassium as they do nitrogen, which is three to four times the amount of phosphorus used.

The majority of soils contain most of their potassium in a relatively unavailable form— the percentage may be as high as 98 percent. The remaining 1 or 2 percent may not be sufficient, although some western soils seem to provide adequate amounts. It should also be noted that the potassium available in the soil is subject to leaching—a fact that should be taken into consideration in container gardening, especially when a lightweight, fast-draining soil mix is used.

Because potassium may be leached from the soil, annual applications should be made in sufficient quantities to supply the plant's needs.

Moderate deficiencies of potassium are difficult to detect in home gardens. The usual symptom is a general reduction in growth, which is not easy to see unless you can compare the size of the plants with others that are growing in a similar place and are getting enough potassium. Furthermore, this may be a symptom of some other nutrient deficiencies. When potassium deficiency becomes severe, applications of potassium cannot correct the damage already done, especially in short-season, fast-growing annuals and vegetables.

The best way to avoid potassium deficiencies is to follow a general fertilization procedure (see page 68), using a complete fertilizer. As a primary nutrient, potassium is a component of all such fertilizers. Potassium is also sold in simple fertilizers, such as sulfate of potash (0-0-52) or muriate of potash (0-0-60).

Because one of the most apparent signs of a potassium deficiency in plants is a general slowing of growth, it is difficult to tell if a plant is suffering from such a deficiency unless you can compare it to a similar plant that is growing normally. In this photograph, the leaf on the left is from a healthy plant; the other two leaves indicate a plant's potassium deficiency.

primarily as a soil amendment, and has a lower nutrient content (approximately 2-3-0). There is some question as to the long-term effect of using sewage sludge products in the garden, particularly around edible crops. Heavy metals, such as cadmium are sometimes present in the sludge, and may build up in the soil. Possible negative effects vary, not only with the origin of the sludge, but also with the characteristics of the soil it is used on.

Legumes as living nitrogen factories

In talking about organic forms of fertilizer nutrients, one should not overlook a natural phenomenon known as nitrogen fixation. The process involves a symbiotic relationship between leguminous plants and various strains of *Rhizobium* bacteria found in the soil.

Nitrogen absorbed and "fixed" into plant-usable forms by bacteria is a very important source of organic nitrogen. For centuries, the bacteria that live on the roots of legumes such as clovers and alfalfa were the principal way (except for manures) to add nitrogen to soil. In parts of New Zealand where clovers grow the year round, bacteria living on the roots will supply all the nitrogen needs of some crops for a full season.

These bacteria are uniquely able to absorb gaseous nitrogen from the air in the soil and show up as nodules on the root system. In some cases, they fix far more than they need themselves, so have plenty to share and leave behind when they die.

Of course there are many different kinds of bacteria, and some are more efficient at nitrogen fixation than others. Also, certain bacteria prefer certain plants (including certain nonleguminous plants) and grow little if at all on others.

The bacteria on the roots of alfalfa are usually the most nitrogen-productive. Following alfalfa, in descending order of nitrogen production, are ladino clover, sweet clover, red clover, kudzu, and white clover. Although these are the most productive nitrogen fixers we know, many other bacteria that live in the soil or on plant roots have the ability to capture and use nitrogen from air.

Green manures

Green manures are also known as cover crops. In contrast to crops grown for their fruit or flower, cover crops are grown for the express purpose of being tilled back into the soil. Tilling these crops into the soil has the effect of improving the physical structure of the soil, increasing the organic matter content, and increasing the soil's fertility.

Cover cropping is a common practice on large commercial farms and ranches, but as noted on page 44, the use of cover crops can also benefit the home gardener in re-establishing topsoils. In addition to the preceding crops listed as nitrogen-fixers, the following crops make excellent green manures in the geographical areas listed. In the northern states: ryegrass (*Lolium multiflorum*); in the southern states, crimson clover (*Trifolium incarnatum*), horse bean (*Vicia faba*), and rough pea (*Lathyrus hirsutus*); in the West, bitter vetch (*Vichia ervilia*) and common vetch (*V. sativa*).

To maximize nutrient return, cover crops should be tilled into the soil shortly before the crop reaches full maturity. If grown on soils of very low fertility, an application of a commercial fertilizer during the growing season will greatly improve growth of the crop and its eventual benefit to the soil.

Nitrogen is "fixed" in the root systems of certain plants within the nodules. The process involves a symbiotic relationship between the plant and specific strains of bacteria in the soil.

This garden plot was planted with a cover crop in the fall and rototilled under the following spring. This process returns nutrients and organic matter from the plants back into the soil.

The end result of individual compost piles will differ widely according to what originally went into the making of the pile. While it rarely is considered a complete fertilizer, compost frequently contains essential nutrients for plant growth and is, of course, an excellent soil amendment.

Compost as Fertilizer?

Albert Howard was a British colonist in India who learned from his surroundings. As a scientist at the 300-acre farm of the Indore Institute of Plant Industry, he developed large-scale composting operations designed after Indian and Chinese folk techniques. Howard returned to England in 1931, after 30 years in India, to spread the word on composting. To this day, the "Indore method" remains the standard by which experts on composting build their heaps, and Sir Albert is venerated as the founder of the "organic" movement.

That Albert Howard was so successful at convincing others of what he considered to be the only natural method of gardening is a tribute to his personal forcefulness, if not his originality. Long before he started the campaign for "organic" methods in England, Yankee farmers were composting

in essentially the same manner. The Americans called the end-product of composting "manure," while Howard called it "humus."

Mature humus is somewhat like horse manure in that it is a conglomerate of partially decomposed (oxidized) vegetable matter. A horse takes nutrients from grasses and other foods, then with the help of bacteria along its digestive tract, the products of metabolic decay are excreted in combination with undecomposed cellulose and certain other relatively stable organic substances.

Within a compost pile (see page 46), microorganisms attack organic matter, breaking it down and producing nitrates and ammonia from nitrogen-containing wastes. Given sufficient oxygen, the amount of available nitrogen may be the factor that limits the rate at which the populations of microorganisms bloom. Hence, urine-soaked ma-

nure and green plant matter are particularly good components. If the starting materials lack sufficient nitrogen, a few handfuls of a high-nitrogen commercial fertilizer sprinkled into the heap will help get the process going.

The whole point of composting, of course, is to produce a beneficial soil additive; and nitrate-production is one of the most obvious benefits. Moreover, humus is recognized by all schools of agricultural thought as an excellent soil conditioner.

However, compost is rarely a complete fertilizer. Depending on the starting materials and the length of time it is allowed to stand before it is applied to the soil, compost may or may not be a good source of the trace elements necessary for plant growth. The same is true for the macronutrients, which are leached from compost if it is allowed to stand unsheltered in the rain.

Fertilizer burn

Throughout this chapter we have talked about the salts contained in fertilizers and fertilizer burn. It's easy to take these terms for granted, but it only takes a couple of errors in the rate of application to realize how quickly you can damage or kill plants, including lawns, with too much fertilizer.

The cause of fertilizer burn is not often understood by most gardeners. William Knoop, Assistant Professor of Horticulture at Iowa State University, explains the phenomenon:

"Fertilizers contain salts. These salts are not unlike table salt except that they contain various plant nutrients. When a salt is added to water the osmotic pressure of the solution is increased. Osmotic pressure is, in a sense, a measure of how tightly water is held in a solution. When a fertilizer, either as a solid or a liquid, is applied to the surface of the soil, the fertilizer salts must sooner or later enter and become part of the soil solution before the nutrients can enter the roots and be used by the plant. The increase in the osmotic pressure of the soil solution associated with the application of a fertilizer may determine whether the plant will sur-

If you think you have applied too much fertilizer, or are concerned about salt build-up within a pot, the excess fertilizer or salts can be *leached* out. Simply run a hose in the pot on low pressure for 10-15 minutes, and the excess materials will be carried out.

vive or will die from a fertilizer burn.

"For a plant's root system to take in water, the water must pass through a root cell membrane. Water can pass through this membrane only when the osmotic pressure of the solution inside the cell is higher than the osmotic pressure of the soil solution outside the cell. Water moves from a solution with low osmotic pressure into a solution with higher osmotic pressure. If the osmotic pressure of the soil solution becomes higher than that of the solution inside the cell, water cannot enter the cell and may even move out of it. This results in the death of the cell. When root cells die, the whole plant may die. The end result is termed a 'fertilizer burn'.

"An understanding of the potential salt effect of the various fertilizer materials can help prevent possible fertilizer burn. Salt index values are a measure of a material's relative tendency to increase the osmotic pressure of the soil solution as compared with the increase caused by an equal weight of sodium nitrate. The salt index of sodium nitrate is 100. The higher the salt index, the greater the potential of a material to increase the osmotic pressure of the soil solution and thus the potential for burn. As indicated in the charts on page 59, there are wide differences in the salt

Organic/Synthetic Sample Comparisons

This table shows the approximate nutrient content of manures, the analysis of a few representative fertilizers, and suggested yearly rates of application per 1000 square feet of garden area. (The rates given are for materials used singly. If combinations of two or more materials are used, reduce the rate accordingly.)

Type of Manure or Fertilizer	Percentage*			Suggested Amounts of Material (pounds) per 1000 sq. feet of garden area
	Nitrogen (N)	Phosphorus (P_2O_5)	Potassium (K_2O)	
chicken manure, dry	2 to 4.5	4.6 to 6.0	1.2 to 2.4	125
steer manure, dry	1 to 2.5	0.9 to 1.6	2.4 to 3.6	450
dairy manure, dry	0.6 to 2.1	0.7 to 1.1	2.4 to 3.6	600
calcium nitrate (15.5-0-0)	15.5	0	0	16 to 25
ammonium sulfate (21-0-0)	21	0	0	12 to 19
ammonium nitrate (33.5-0-0)	33.5	0	0	7 to 12
urea (46-0-0)	46	0	0	5 to 9
5-10-10	5	10	10	30 to 40
16-20-0	16	20	0	16 to 25
16-16-16	16	16	16	15 to 25

*P_2O_5 actually contains only 44 percent phosphorus, and K_2O contains only 83 percent potassium. The percentages given for the oxide may be converted to percentages of the element by multiplication: $P_2O_5 \times 0.44 = P$; $K_2O \times 0.83 = K$.

indexes of those fertilizer materials used.

"The salt index of a fertilizer material is extremely important, especially when the fertilizer is highly soluble [see page 60-61]. The rates of application must be lower when a fertilizer with a high salt index is used, basically because of the salt effect.

"Fertilizers with a low salt index should be used when soil test results indicate the presence of excessive levels of soluble salts in the soil."

Synthetic Fertilizers.

Although you would not guess it from the number and diversity of the fertilizer products on the market, the amount of information any gardener needs to know concerning commercially available fertilizers is relatively limited and basic. All fertilizer products have a great deal in common.

The first step is to understand the label. All commercial fertilizers are labeled with the percentages they contain of nitrogen, phosphate and potash—the macronutrients. There are many formulations—24-4-8, 5-10-10, 12-6-6, 16-16-16 and so on— but the listings are always in the same order, with nitrogen first, followed by phosphate, and potash last—note the alphabetical order. Even fertilizers which are not complete, that is, those containing only one or two of the primary elements, are still labeled the same: for example, 0-10-10, 0-20-0, 21-0-0, 0-0-60, etc. These products have special uses which are discussed on page 64.

At this point, one general rule can be established: The percentage of nitrogen in the formula usually dictates the amount of fertilizer to be applied.

Not only do fertilizers come in different formulations, they come in many different forms: dry, liquid, slow-release, organic, pelleted and soluble, to name a few.

Why all the different formulations and forms? This has a lot to do with the personal habits of gardeners. Different liquid, dry or slow-release fertilizers may all have the same percentages of nitrogen, phosphate and potash,

and even the same micronutrients. But one gardener will prefer the dry fertilizer to mix in with a soil mix, while another wants to mix the liquid in a hose sprayer and feed the entire yard at once, while the hanging-basket specialist wants to fertilize as few times as possible and uses a slow-release form. There's a discussion of the various types and forms of fertilizers on pages 64 and 65.

The number of different formulations available is the product of research into the specific needs of specific plants. While there are a great many plants that do not have such specific needs, there are many which will give the gardener superior results only when they are given some special care, including a "customized" fertilizer. Many of the plants that have special fertilizer requirements are also particular about their soil and water requirements. These plants are grouped together in the section called Special Handling, starting on page 85.

The label and the law

For many years there has been a model label law which many states have adopted for the classification of fertilizers, establishing minimum levels of nutrients allowable, and specific labeling requirements. To date, model legislation has not met with total acceptance, and so there are still differences from state to state as to what constitutes a fertilizer, and the type of information on labels.

Even so, the information contained on fertilizer labels has been quite well standardized, and the consumer is protected by state laws requiring manufacturers to guarantee the claimed nutrients.

Most often the label will state the percentages of nitrogen, phosphate and potash, and the sources of those nutrients. In some fertilizers you'll find a secondary nutrient (calcium, magnesium and/or sulfur) listed along with the primary nutrients. And some manufacturers will also include the micronutrients on the label.

The law requires only that the manufacturer guarantee what is claimed on the label, so in some cases, a fertilizer will contain secondary nutrients or micronutrients not listed on the label because the manufacturer does not want to guarantee their exact amounts. But the gardener-consumer can rest assured that what is stated on the label is actually contained in the fertilizer.

Salt Index Chart
Salt values for commonly used nitrogen fertilizer materials.
(Note: the last column is the practical measure of relative saltiness.)

Material	Approx. % N	Salt Index	Salt effect per 10 lb. nutrient
Ammonium Nitrate	33	105	1.49
Ammonium Sulfate	21	69	1.63
Calcium Nitrate	15.5	69	2.23
I.B.D.U	30	5	0.08
Potassium Nitrate	14	74	2.67
Natural Organic	5	4	0.40
UF	38	10	0.13
Urea	45	75	0.81

Salt values for other commonly used materials.

Material	Approx. Nutrient Level	Salt Index	Salt effect per 10 lb. nutrient
Superphosphate	20% P_2O_5	8	0.20
Potassium Chloride	60% K_2O	114	0.87
Potassium Sulfate	50% K_2O	46	0.43
Dolomite	30% CaO 20% MgO	1	—
Gypsum	33% CaO	8	0.12
Epsom Salts	16% MgO	44	1.38

Where Does It Come From?

Scrutinizing a fertilizer label can tell you a great deal about the nature of the contents inside the bottle or bag. On these four pages we will give you the know-how to decipher information offered on almost every plant food label. The sample label to the right is like none you will ever run across; it is a combination of many types of labels.

The information on these pages can be of considerable importance to gardeners because the source of the nutrients, particularly nitrogen, will, to a large extent, determine how the nutrients react in the soil and their subsequent availability to plants.

Nitrogen

In Germany about 1910, the means for economical chemical fixation of nitrogen into ammonia was worked out, primarily by the scientist Fritz Haber. Later refined by a Frenchman, Georges Claude, the *Claude-Haber Process* still represents the least expensive effort of technology to "fix" nitrogen. Simply put, nitrogen and hydrogen are reacted under very high temperatures and pressure to form ammonia. Much of the ammonia so synthesized is liquefied under pressure and tremendous quantities of the liquid are used by the agricultural industry, applied directly to the soil with the aid of special tools and equipment.

Ammoniacal nitrogen: acidifying and non-leachable

Anhydrous ammonia, the product of the Claude-Haber process, is the starting point for the following forms of ammoniacal nitrogen. Note: Exact formulas may vary

ammonium sulfate	$(NH_4)_2SO_4$	21-0-0
ammonium nitrate	NH_4NO_3	34-0-0
urea	$CO(NH_2)_2$	46-0-0
monoammonium phosphate	$NH_4H_2PO_4$	11-48-0
diammonium phosphate	$(NH_4)_2HPO_4$	21-53-0

---

1 General Purpose Plant Food

2 8-8-8

3 GUARANTEED ANALYSIS:

4 Total Nitrogen (N) 8%

5
- 3.1% Ammoniacal Nitrogen
- 1.2% Urea Nitrogen
- 2.4% Nitrate Nitrogen
- 1.3% Water Insoluble Nitrogen

6 Available Phosphoric Acid (P_2O_5) 8%

7 Soluble Potash (K_2O) 8%

8 Primary Nutrients from Ammonium Sulfate, Urea, Ammonium Phosphates, Sulfate of Potash, and Muriate of Potash.

9
- Calcium (Ca) 1.5%
- Magnesium (Mg) 1.0%
- Sulfur (S) 4.5%
- Iron (Fe) 0.2%
- Manganese (Mn) 0.08%
- Zinc (Zn) 0.09%

10 Secondary and Trace Nutrients from Dolomitic Limestone, Ammonium Sulfate, Sulfate of Potash, Iron Sulfate, Manganese Oxide, and Zinc Oxide.

11 Potential Acidity 400 lbs. Calcium Carbonate Equivalent per ton.

1) In this example, "General Purpose Plant Food" is the equivalent of a brand name. **2)** The formula, grade or analysis, these numbers are the percentages of nitrogen, phosphate, and potash (always in that order) of the contents. **3)** The manufacturer's warranty that the stated analysis is present in the container. The guaranteed analysis is always stated in this order and form. **4)** This is the sum total of the percentages of nitrogen from the listed sources. **5)** These percentages are not required in every case, but most manufacturers supply this information. The source of the nitrogen is important because, in many respects, the source governs the way the nitrogen reacts in the soil. **(6&7)** The percentages of the other two primary nutrients are listed only if their presence is claimed elsewhere on the label. **8)** The sources of the three primary nutrients. In most cases the sources are basic fertilizers which, when combined, make a "complete" fertilizer. **9)** Percentages of secondary and micronutrients may be present in many fertilizers, but they are not always claimed on the label. If percentages *are* indicated, the manufacturer is guaranteeing those amounts. **10)** Sources of the secondary and micronutrients. **11)** Some fertilizers have an acid reaction in the soil. If this potential exists, the label will indicate the number of pounds of calcium carbonate (laboratory quality limestone) it would take to completely neutralize the acidity of the fertilizer once it was in the soil.

---

somewhat by manufacturer. Numbers given are approximate.

All of these are available to home gardeners either in the forms named above or as sources of "primary nutrients" in many familiar fertilizers as seen in the sample label above.

Ammoniacal fertilizers have a gradual acidifying effect on soils. The nitrogen contained in these fertilizers stays in the root zone longer than nitrate nitrogen, because of its chemical composition. It does not readily leach from the soil. The ammoniacal forms of nitrogen undergo nitrification—to nitrate—to become the most common form in the soil. This nitrification process is facilitated by soil microorganisms which, in turn, are dependent on warm soil for greatest activity. Ammoniacal nitrogen, therefore, is indirectly dependent on soil temperature for availability to plants. In warm soils, this nitrification will be largely complete within 3 weeks. In cold or sterile soils, it will take much longer.

Ammonium sulfate is very widely used and commonly available. It is the most acidifying and has a fairly high salt index compared with the other common ammonia fertilizers.

Urea is the most concentrated nitrogen fertilizer normally available to home gardeners. Even though urea is a product of ammoniacal nitrogen, because of its chemical composition it has a comparatively low salt index. Some states allow urea to be marketed as an "organic" fertilizer. It is quite acid-forming and, whether in the dry or liquid form, is usually applied with water.

Ammonium nitrate has some of the qualities of both ammoniacal nitrogen and nitrate nitrogen. Because it is basically fast acting, it is grouped with the nitrates.

Ammonium phosphate and diammonium phosphate are also carriers of ammoniacal nitrogen, but because they supply more phosphorus than nitrogen, we have listed them with the other phosphorus fertilizers on page 62.

Nitrates: fast-acting and leachable

The first widely available inorganic nitrogen fertilizer was a nitrate. Called Chilean nitrate (16-0-0), it was first mined in the early 1800s in a desert valley in Chile that has vast natural deposits of remarkably pure sodium nitrate ($NaNO_3$).

Chilean or sodium nitrate is used relatively little today. Although a little is commercially synthesized and used to some extent in the southeastern United States, sodium nitrate is now only interesting history in most other areas.

Basically, nitrate fertilizers are made by reacting ammonia (NH_3) with oxygen (O_2) to form nitric acid (HNO_3). This acid is then chemically manipulated to produce the various nitrate fertilizers.

The more important nitrate fertilizers today are:

ammonium nitrate	NH_4NO_3	34-0-0
calcium nitrate	$Ca(NO_3)_2$	15-0-0
potassium nitrate	KNO_3	14-0-35

Ammonium nitrate is by far the most widely used of these three.

Nitrate fertilizers are quick to dissolve in water and the nitrate ion (NO_3-) is already in a form plants can use—no microbial action is necessary. Therefore nitrate fertilizers are not inhibited by cold or sterile soils.

Unlike ammoniacal nitrogen, nitrate nitrogen does not become attached to soil particles, so it is easily washed by rains or heavy watering deep into the soil, sometimes past the reach of roots.

Nitrate fertilizers are not acid forming. (Ammonium nitrate is one exception but because of the ammonium, not the nitrate.) In fact, both calcium nitrate and potassium nitrate have an overall basic reaction, slightly raising soil pH in some cases.

The main points to remember about nitrate nitrogen are that it is fast acting, readily soluble, can be easily leached from the soil, does not have an acidifying effect and is not dependent on soil microorganisms for availability to the plant.

Water-insoluble nitrogen: improved efficiency, greater convenience

Water-insoluble nitrogen fertilizers are, in varying degrees, slow-release fertilizers. Because they make nitrogen available over a comparatively long period of time, efficiency is their virtue, especially when compared with soluble formulations. In some cases, 30 to 40 percent of the nitrogen supplied by a soluble chemical fertilizer is leached away before the plant's roots can absorb it.

Whether the plant is an annual or perennial, the quantity of fertilizer applied at one time, and timing are factors that will affect how much is actually used. Nevertheless, the ideal fertilizer is one that would release only as much nutrient as necessary when the plant needs it. Slow-release fertilizers seek to do just that.

The rate of nutrient release is slowed in three main ways. Most simply, pellets of relatively insoluble fertilizer are made larger than normal, preventing too rapid a breakdown by soil microorganisms. MagAmp, a popular slow-release fertilizer, is available in a "coarse" grade that will release nutrients for over two years, and in a finer, faster-acting form.

Another way manufacturers slow the release rate of a fertilizer is to change it chemically, rendering a portion insoluble. Urea has been modified in this way to make ureaform (the same as urea-formaldehyde and Nitroform) and IBDU. Both are variations of the same fertilizer, urea.

Ureaform is 38 percent nitrogen (38-0-0), 70 percent of which is water-insoluble nitrogen, abbreviated W.I.N. The rate of release of the W.I.N. portion is fastest when microbial activity in the soil is greatest.

IBDU also contains 38 percent nitrogen of which 90 percent is W.I.N. The release of the W.I.N. is affected by the moisture content of the soil and the size of individual fertilizer particles—smaller

The process of manufacturing synthetic fertilizers is a complex one, involving much technology. The results have been the increased availability of many convenient forms of fertilizers, at reduced cost to farmers and gardeners alike.

ones release first. IBDU is less dependent on soil microorganisms than ureaform.

Ureaform and IBDU are used primarily for lawn fertilization. Many typical lawn fertilizers show on the label "Percent W.I.N." Usually ureaform is used for this purpose.

Authorities have decided that if less than 15 percent (by weight) of the nitrogen in a fertilizer is water insoluble (W.I.N.), the fertilizer is basically fast-acting. If between 15 and 30 percent is insoluble, it is medium-acting, and any with more than 30 percent insoluble nitrogen is basically a slow-acting fertilizer.

A slow-acting fertilizer is much less likely to burn the lawn after application and is much less subject to being flushed from the soil by water.

The third important type of slow-release fertilizer is essentially a soluble liquid fertilizer wrapped in a small plastic pill. Although these plastic shells are thin and can be easily broken between the fingers, the soluble fertilizers inside are gradually emitted under normal garden circumstances.

Expensive to buy, this kind of fertilizer has become very popular with growers of potted plants and hanging baskets. Soluble kinds are quickly leached from containers, so need constant replenishment.

These also are available as complete fertilizers and in several balanced formulas.

Other slow release fertilizers

There are slow-release fertilizers not discussed here. For instance, many organic fertilizers are essentially slow release. As a general rule, they will release about half of the nutrients they contain through the first growing season.

Slow-release fertilizers are more expensive but against that, weigh less waste and more convenience.

Convenience and labor saving are factors because instead of applying a soluble fertilizer every week, month, or however often the label directs, enough slow-release for the entire growing season can be applied at one time in some cases.

Slow-release fertilizers are not salty. This reduces the chance of fertilizer "burn."

3.1% Ammoniacal Nitrogen	
1.2% Urea Nitrogen	
2.4% Nitrate Nitrogen	
1.3% Water Insoluble Nitrogen	
Available Phosphoric Acid (P_2O_5)	**8%**
Soluble Potash (K_2O)	**8%**
Primary Nutrients from Ammonium Sulfate, Urea, Ammonium Phosphates, Sulfate of Potash, and Muriate of Potash.	
Calcium (Ca)	1.5%
Magnesium (Mg)	1.0%
Sulfur (S)	4.5%

Phosphorus

By the 1800s, phosphorus was known to be essential to plant growth. The only common sources of the mineral—bones and rock phosphate—were very insoluble. Then it was discovered that treating either bones or rock phosphate with sulfuric acid increased the solubility, hence availability to plants, and the phosphorus industry was off and running. Today the most common phosphorus fertilizer—ordinary superphosphate—is manufactured by treating rock phosphate with sulfuric acid. Following are descriptions of each.

Rock phosphate. A natural, mined mineral, the actual percentage phosphorus will vary according to the source. It is mined in many locations throughout the U.S. and world. The phosphate content ranges between 27 and 41 percent (0-27-0, 0-41-0).

Rock phosphate is most useful on acid soils low in phosphorus. Even in those cases, it should be applied in quantities two to three times greater than recommended for superphosphate.

For short season plants that need phosphorus, rock phosphate is too slowly available to be of much use.

In soils with a pH above 7, the rock phosphate will become available so slowly it is of negligible value.

Guano. The waste product of sea birds and bats, guano was at one time a very important fertilizer. It typically contains about 9 percent water-soluble phosphate as well as 13 percent nitrogen. The phosphorus contained in guano is a very soluble form plants can use.

Unfortunately guano supplies

are finite and the richest deposits have already been depleted. It is still available in limited quantities.

Ordinary superphosphate. Superphosphate, 0-20-0, is rock phosphate treated with sulfuric acid to make it more soluble. It also contains calcium and sulfur, both essential nutrients.

Used alone, it is a good phosphorus source. Approximately 90 percent is water-soluble. A large quantity of superphosphate is used to manufacture dry, powdered or granular complete fertilizers.

Concentrated superphosphate. Rock phosphate is the initial ingredient as with ordinary superphosphate, but the gypsum is removed from the reaction products. The resulting fertilizer is almost 98 percent water soluble and has a formula of 0-45-0.

This is the most concentrated form of phosphorus normally available to home gardeners. The convenience of greater concentration is an advantage; however, it includes little additional sulfur. A prime use is for the manufacture of mixed complete fertilizers.

Ammonium phosphates. These are made by combining ammonia with phosphoric acid. The most common kinds are monoammonium phosphate (MAP) 11-48-0 and diammonium phosphate (DAP) 21-53-0, or mixtures of the two—16-48-0 and 18-46-0.

Generally, the phosphorus content of these fertilizers is equally available with ordinary or concentrated superphosphate. Also, they have the advantage of supplying nitrogen at the same time. These will dissolve in water and will have an overall acid reaction in the soil because of the ammonium component. Ammonium phosphates are widely used in the manufacture of complete fertilizers.

Phosphorus fertilizers. Vegetables and other short season plants generally are best fertilized with more water soluble phosphates such as ordinary or concentrated superphosphate. Water solubility is less important to longer-lived plants with more extensive root systems.

Water insoluble rock phosphate will be much more effective if it is finely ground or powdered and mixed thoroughly into the soil.

Potassium

Potassium, also called potash, is absorbed by plants in very large quantities, more than any other mineral except nitrogen.

The exact function of potassium in plants has not yet been specifically pinned down. Nevertheless,

...al Nitrog...	
3.1% Ammoniacal Nitrogen	
1.2% Urea Nitrogen	
2.4% Nitrate Nitrogen	
1.3% Water Insoluble Nitrogen	
Available Phosphoric Acid (P_2O_5)	8%
Soluble Potash (K_2O)	**8%**
Primary Nutrients from Ammonium Sulfate, Urea, Ammonium Phosphates, Sulfate of Potash, and Muriate of Potash.	
Calcium (Ca)	1.5%
Magnesium (Mg)	1.0%
Sulfur (S)	4.5%

it has been observed that a plant's structural strength is greater with a good potassium supply. Winter hardiness and disease resistance of some plants, lawns for instance, are improved if potassium is abundant.

Processing potassium ore, unlike phosphorus, is a matter of purification, not increasing solubility.

Muriate of potash, potassium

chloride (0-0-60) is by far the most common and, hence, least expensive. Two other sources of potassium worth noting are potassium sulfate (0-0-50) and potassium nitrate (13-0-44).

Potassium chloride is the most salty of the above. Also some plants, citrus for instance, are sensitive to excess chloride. Potassium sulfate is used primarily in crops that can't take the chloride.

Potassium nitrate is relatively expensive to make so is not used much. It is a good non-chloride potassium fertilizer and supplies nitrate nitrogen as well.

All potassium fertilizers easily dissolve in water and are immediately available to the plant. In use, they may be applied directly mixed into the soil, dissolved and applied as a liquid, or used in the manufacture of mixed fertilizers.

Is any one kind of fertilizer best?
If you've read straight through these pages you might be wondering about such a question. Unfortunately, there is no true answer all the time, in all situations.

From the preceding descriptions of various fertilizers, it's evident each has advantages and disadvantages.

If you're like most gardeners, and have different kinds of plants in all kinds of situations—lawns, container plants, acid lovers, bonsai—you'll eventually want to have on hand the fertilizers that work best for you in each situation. While there isn't one fertilizer that works best in all gardening situations, there are some which work better for specific plants than others. The previous information combined with your own experience should help you discover which fertilizers work the best for you, in the shortest possible time.

After underground mining of potassium, the mineral is purified and converted into several forms of potassium, or potash fertilizer.

Common Fertilizer Forms

Simple or single nutrient fertilizers

Pro: (for the knowledgeable practitioner): Because these fertilizers are relatively inexpensive, very concentrated and take little storage space, experienced gardeners find them most practical when a specific nutrient is needed.

Con: Because they are concentrated and often highly soluble, it's easier to damage plants by applying too much—especially nitrogen fertilizers. Other nutrient needs may be easily overlooked. The incomplete fertilizers are most useful if you know—on the basis of a soil test or plant symptoms—the specific nutrient that is lacking.

Popular examples: nitrogen fertilizers such as ammonium sulfate (21-0-0) and urea (46-0-0) are common. Superphosphate (0-20-0), triple superphosphate (0-46-0), ammonium nitrate (34-0-0) and muriate of potash (0-0-60) are also widely available. Almost always sold in dry form.

Slow-release fertilizers

Pro: These are the labor-saving fertilizers. More can be applied at one time, reducing the frequency of feedings. Further, the feeding is gradual so plants are not shocked as is possible from a too heavy application of soluble fertilizer.

Con: Cost is a factor—slow-release fertilizers are always more expensive. Some are activated to release nutrients by water, others by warm soil temperatures. Therefore the rate of nutrient release is not constant and somewhat unpredictable, and may be too slow during periods of rapid growth.

Popular examples: Osmocote—available in two formulas: 14-14-14 lasts 3 to 4 months and 18-6-12 lasts 8 to 9 months. Activated by soil temperature and microbial activity. Used by commercial growers of container plants.

MagAmp—one formula, 7-40-0, available in two grades. Coarse grade lasts 2 years, medium 1 year. Used by commercial growers of container plants.

IBDU—slow-release lawn fertilizer. Contained in some lawn fertilizers, straight IBDU is 30-0-0. Nitrogen release is dependent primarily upon soil moisture, soil pH, and particle size.

Ureaform—commonly added to lawn fertilizers to increase gradual, long-lasting feeding of nitrogen. Straight ureaform is 38-0-0. See Water-insoluble nitrogen, page 61. Some complete fertilizers contain ureaform and are referred to as "timed-release" products. Their breakdown is dependent upon microbial activity, and their effectiveness lasts from three to six months. ORTHO's Pot and Planter Food and African Violet Food 6-9-5 are examples.

Use: MagAmp and Osmocote are widely available and popular with container and hanging basket gardeners. Ureaform and IBDU are primarily used by lawn owners for slow and gradual turf fertilizing.

Fertilizers combined with insecticides or herbicides

Pro: Convenience is the great advantage of these products. On lawns, for example, in one pass with a spreader they can fertilize the grass and kill the weeds. For many gardeners, this is much simpler than buying an herbicide, mixing it and then spraying the weeds.

Con: Proper timing is the main problem. The best time to fertilize is not always the best time to control weeds. For use only when a problem exists that needs pesticide.

Popular examples: ORTHO's Weed and Feed for lawns, Systemic Rose & Flower Care and Crab Grass Control Plus Lawn Food 18-3-6. Any good-size garden center will offer a wide variety. "Weed and Feed" may be printed large on the bag or there will be other words to indicate that the contents of the bag do more than just fertilize. Read the label carefully and follow the directions, observing all cautions.

Use: These combination products are available for two of the most demanding plants in the garden: roses and lawn grasses. Many fertilizer/insecticide/herbicide combinations exist for specific rose or lawn problems.

Soluble complete fertilizers

Pro: Because these fertilizers are theoretically 100 percent soluble in water, all the nutrients they contain are ready immediately for the plant's use. They come as dry crystals or in concentrated solutions. The effects of application closely follow application. Nutrient availability from these fertilizers is less dependent on warmer temperatures, so they can be used in early spring while soils are still cool.

Con: These fertilizers can be misused. The gardener must be conscientious, following the label directions closely. A dose too strong can "burn" leaves. Used too infrequently, the plants will starve in between feedings.

Popular examples: Hyponex, RapidGro, Spoonit, Miracid, ORTHO's House Plant Food 5-10-5 and ORTHO-GRO Liquid Plant Food 12-6-6 are all widely available examples of this type of fertilizer. Specific formulations vary and there are special formulations for plants with specific needs (such as lawns or orchids or ferns).

Use: Because of their complete solubility, these fertilizers are often used for hydroponics. They are also useful for container gardening where frequent waterings leach out nutrients. To compensate for the leaching, these fertilizers are applied more frequently but at lower concentrations than the insoluble complete fertilizers.

Natural organic fertilizers

Pro: improving soil structure and slow release of plant nutrients, (thereby reducing the danger of over-fertilizing) are the two most outstanding benefits of using organic fertilizers. The extent of these effects will vary depending upon the type of fertilizer you use. In some rural areas, natural organic fertilizers, such as manures, are readily available and often free for the taking.

Con: Comparing nutrient cost with synthetic fertilizers, commercially available organics may be expensive. Because a considerable quantity is usually needed, they are bulky and difficult to handle. The effectiveness of organic fertilizers is dependent upon warm soil temperatures and a vigorous population of soil microbes—these variables reduce predictability. Also, some manures should be used with caution: They may be too salty, weed-seed carriers, or too "hot" (see page 58).

Popular examples: Manures make excellent organic fertilizers and soil conditioners. Blood meal and fish emulsion are relatively easiest to handle, although —when compared with synthetic formulations on a nutrient-by-nutrient basis—they are relatively expensive. Sewage sludge, activated or composted, is becoming increasingly available. Bone meal is an excellent source of phosphorus. Composts will vary widely depending upon what goes into them. Few are useful as fertilizers.

Use: There is a natural organic fertilizer for almost every garden need. Liquid forms, such as Ortho's Fish Emulsion Fertilizer 5-1-1, are widely used in container gardening. Compost and manures are successfully used on lawns, roses and vegetables.

Partially soluble complete fertilizers

Pro: These are the fertilizers most often used for general garden purposes. Many formulations for specific groups of plants exist: rose food, vegetable garden food, orchid food, citrus food, lawn food, houseplant food, and so on. They supply in one application the mineral elements plants need most—nitrogen, phosphorus and potassium. Because of their partial insolubility, they will supply some nutrients over a longer period of time than the soluble complete fertilizers do.

Con: The individual nutrients are usually less concentrated, hence the nutrient cost per pound may be higher than for simple or single nutrient fertilizers. For low analysis products, it is necessary to buy and apply more pounds of fertilizer.

Popular examples: ORTHO's Vegetable Garden Food 5-10-10 and General Purpose Plant Food 8-8-8, and many other brands are available in every conceivable form—liquid, dry, slow-release, spikes, pellets, tablets, granules, etc. There are similarities, however. High nitrogen kinds, such as 24-4-8, are recommended for lawns. High phosphorus types, such as 6-18-6, are recommended as starter fertilizers. Between these examples are the many special-purpose complete fertilizers.

Use: These are the workhorses of garden fertilizers. More gardeners use them on more plants than any other form of fertilizer. Growers of annuals—vegetables or flowers—favor these as pre-plant fertilizers that provide at least the three major nutrients over a comparatively long period of time.

Organic Gardening A Misnomer?

by Wesley P. Judkins
Professor Emeritus of Horticulture
Virginia Polytechnic Institute & State University
Blacksburg, Virginia and
Floyd F. Smith
Research Entomologist
USDA Agricultural Research Center
Beltsville, Maryland
This article originally appeared in the 1979 U.S. Dept. of
Agriculture Yearbook and American Horticulturist
Magazine. It is reprinted by permission of the authors.

As a part of our present concern for a cleaner, more healthful environment, the use of organic foods is being promoted as a means to this end. This subject deserves the serious attention of all consumers because, if such foods are superior to those which are usually eaten, we should all adjust our menus and include more of these items.

The designation "organic food" is actually a misnomer because all foods are in fact organic — except for an extremely small amount of preservatives or flavoring components. The term organic food refers to foods which are produced without the use of inorganic chemical fertilizers, pesticides, preservatives, or flavoring ingredients. The organic enthusiast considers inorganic chemicals to be harmful to both man and his environment.

Foods consumed by the earliest, prehistoric human creatures were truly organic. Men roamed many acres of land to kill wild game, catch fish and gather berries, nuts and other plant parts for food.

The development of modern agriculture

As early man subsisted for many thousands of years by killing and eating wild animals and feeding on plants growing within his vast range of foraging, he filled a niche in the balance of nature. His increase in numbers was limited by the available food which nature supplied. Gradually, as man discovered ways to cultivate some of the wild plants and to domesticate livestock, he increased his available supplies of food. This allowed an increase in population and the establishment of family and tribal units in stable communities.

He soon discovered that the use of manure from livestock and poultry promoted higher yields of his corn and vegetables. Later he found that material from deposits of guano, marl, potash and nitrate of soda also improved crop production. As he acquired a knowledge of chemistry, he learned that nitrogen, phosphorus and potassium were the principal elements he needed to add to the soil to produce better growth. He then learned how to utilize natural deposits more efficiently and to synthesize inorganic commerical fertilizers.

It is this involvement with inorganic chemicals which disturbs the organic enthusiast. Organic compounds are those which contain carbon, whereas inorganic materials do not. The conclusion seems to be that inorganic compounds in general are harmful, whereas organic ones are beneficial.

In reality, we live in a chemical environment in which either type may be harmful or beneficial. Water, which is inorganic, is essential for life. Salt, also inorganic, is essential for most humans, but quite harmful to those with certain medical problems. Sugar, one of the basic organic components of food, is beneficial as a source of energy for most people, but detrimental to the diabetic. Many organic materials in excess may be harmful or deadly such as poison ivy, poisonous mushrooms, alcohol, marijuana, tobacco and heroin. Aflatoxins, complex chemicals produced naturally by certain fungi found on stored food, are the most potent carcinogens known to man. Entry of aflatoxin-producing fungi is encouraged by insects feeding on nuts, fruits and vegetables.

Some facts about organic foods

In considering the advantages and disadvantages of organically and inorganically grown crops, it is necessary to understand how the plant absorbs its nutrient elements and synthe-sizes them into food. Regardless of the original source, fertilizer in the soil must break down into its ionic form before it can be used by plants. The ions, which the plants absorb, are identical whether they are derived from an organic or inorganic source. Therefore, in terms of benefits to plants, when similar quantities of nutrients are available, there is no advantage for either organic or inorganic fertilizer.

Green plants are the initial and ultimate source of human food. It is logical to conclude that, since these plants can absorb their nutrient elements only in the ionic form, the food value of agricultural crops would be identical when they received fertilizer from either inorganic or organic sources. This is, in fact, the case. Experiments conducted at several State and Federal Experiment Stations have found no differences in the mineral or vitamin content of crops grown with organic as compared to inorganic sources of nutrients.

The Benefits of Organic Matter

The home gardener derives several benefits by mulching with organic matter. It reduces erosion caused by runoff of rain or irrigation, increases the infiltration of water into the soil and conserves this moisture by reducing evaporation. An organic mulch helps suppress weed growth.

Some of the best organic materials to use as mulch are leaves, lawn clippings fresh sawdust, fine wood shavings, pine needles, chopped straw, ground corn cobs, shredded tobacco or sugar cane stems, peanut hulls, or cotton seed hulls. These materials do not add important amounts of nutrients or have a significant effect on the pH of the soil.

The dead vegetable and flower plants in your garden should be chopped down and left on the ground as a protective mulch during the winter. This trash mulch reduces erosion and improves the organic matter content of the soil when the garden is prepared for planting in the spring. Corn stalks, tomato vines and other tall plants should be cut into eight inch pieces with a sickle or pruning shears. Chop up low plants like beans and bushy flowers by running along the row with a rotary lawn mower. Unmulched areas in gardens and fields, not occupied by growing crops, should be planted to green manure crops such as rye, ryegrass, millet, sorghum, or crimson clover. They will reduce leaching of nutrients and increase organic matter for the next crop as they are worked into the soil.

Salvaging and recycling organic waste materials

Organic waste materials such as leaves, manure from livestock and poultry and the organic portion of urban trash collections should be salvaged and used as fertilizer, mulch, or compost. Farmers and gardeners should use such materials whenever they are available.

Some cities accumulate leaves in huge piles during fall collection periods. After several months of composting, the material is available at little or no cost to gardeners. This is a practical way to reduce environmental pollution and supply organic material for gardens and farms.

The solid waste from urban areas which is hauled away as garbage to be burned or buried should also be recycled. Processes are now available, and are being used by a limited number of cities, whereby glass, metal and paper are salvaged for use by industry, and the remaining organic portion is utilized to produce heat or is made into compost for crop production. Future generations may justifiably condemn us for wasting these valuable resources.

Losses by insect and disease attack

Probably the greatest deterrent to successful growing of vegetables is the damaging effect or crop loss by insect pests and disease organisms. The severity of damage is greatly influenced by the weather which varies, not only geographically, but fluctuates from year to year in the same region.

Winter temperatures determine how many eggs, pupae, or adult insects survive from autumn to spring. Cool or warm spring weather influences disease infection. Temperature also determines the time of emergence of pests from hibernation, their build up to damaging numbers on early planted crops and the development of parasites and predators of these pests. Prolonged droughts and high summer temperatures kill eggs or other stages of many pests by heat or desiccation. High humidity and rainy periods are favorable for rapid spread of plant diseases, but also enhance disease epidemics that suddenly destroy thriving infestations of aphids or caterpillars.

Time of planting is important in avoiding losses by diseases and pests in certain regions. Since seed corn maggots destroy early planting of beans and corn, you should delay planting until the soil warms. Early maturing varieties of sweet corn can avoid the worst earworm problem. Likewise, delay plantings of summer squash to avoid early season activity and resultant damage by squash vine borer.

Controlling plant diseases

When planning for vegetable production in a home garden or commerical enterprise, consult your local Extension agent or seed catalog for information on disease resistant varieties. Excellent new introductions are available each year and should be selected to improve the efficiency of production, and reduce the need for spraying. Comparable insect resistant varieties have not been developed.

Some vegetable crops are highly subject to damage by pests or disease organisms and require special treatments by experienced growers to insure a crop. Others are relatively pest-free and may require no treatments in some seasons. The beginner should first plant only trouble-free crops, later trying the more difficult ones as he gains experience.

Mechanical control of insects

Attack by cutworms can be prevented by placing a simple collar of stiff paper (cut from a drinking cup or milk carton) around newly set tomato, cabbage and pepper plants — and even sweet corn. The collar should extend about one inch into the soil and two inches above ground.

Slugs that emerge at night from hiding places in wall crevices, loose mulch, piles of plant stakes or trash, can be trapped under pieces of board, shingles or flat stones laid in the garden. Lift them each day and destroy the slugs. Slugs are attracted to shallow vessels partially filled with beer into which they crawl and expire. Slug baits moistened with a teaspoon of beer will be twice as effective.

An aluminum foil mulch around low growing plants reflects the ultraviolet rays from the sky and repels flying insects (including aphids, leafhoppers, thrips, Mexican bean beetles and cucumber beetles) from landing on the plants. Summer squash, Chinese cabbage, lettuce and peppers have been protected from virus infection transmitted by aphid feeding. Roses, gladiolus, beans and cucurbits have been protected from chewing and sucking insects.

Black polyethylene mulches, used extensively by commercial fruit and vegetable growers, help to control weeds, conserve moisture and prevent leaching of fertility in the home garden. They also keep the produce from resting on the soil, thus reducing rot infection from soil contact.

Blacklight traps are frequently advertised for control of insect pests in home gardens and on farms. Although great numbers of moths and other insects are attracted to individual black lights and captured in the attached traps or killed on electric grids, there is little or no reduction of pest insects that attack your vegetables. Sometimes the insect pests in the vicinity of the trap will be greater than normal. Insects attracted to the light may not enter the trap, but linger to lay their eggs in the vicinity. Likewise, certain bait traps, as for the Japanese beetle, may actually increase the infestation in the vicinity of the trap.

Interplanting of vegetables with repellent plants

A recent calendar for home gardeners lists a number of plants that should be planted among your vegetables to deter cabbage worms, Mexican bean beetles, Colorado potato beetles, Japanese beetles, borers and tomato hornworms.

Carefully conducted experiments by research entomologists at State and Federal Experiment Stations have shown no beneficial results from such interplantings except for the reduction of one type of nematode by marigold roots. Moreover, these experiments showed that Mexican bean beetles and Colorado potato beetles found their respective host plants in mixed plantings. Onions and garlic supported thriving populations of onion thrips and mites, and had no measurable repelling effect on cabbage worms, bean beetles, cucumber beetles and aphids that infested their respective interplanted host plants.

Parasites and predators

Few gardeners ever see the most efficient parasites and predators at work among the pests on their plants. Examples of beneficial insects are: the yellow and black banded thrips; the tiny Orius plant bug; syrphid fly larvae; aphis lions — the ugly looking larvae of the delicate lacewing flies; and larvae and adults of our native ladybird beetles that suck the juices from plant-feeding thrips, spider mites, aphids, young caterpillars and leafhoppers.

Often during periods of cool damp weather, epidemics of insect disease, caused by bacteria, fungi, or viruses, will suddenly destroy thriving populations of pests — especially aphids, cabbage worms, cabbage loopers and other caterpillars.

Until recently, the Mexican bean beetle has defoliated beans, lima beans and soy beans over wide areas without the depressing effect of parasites or predators. A tiny wasp was recently introduced from India that lays 10 or more eggs in each bean beetle larva, and soon, the larva turns black and dies. This microscopic parasite disperses for 10 miles or more in search of bean beetle infestations. The parasite does not survive our winters for lack of food, but, if reintroduced each season from laboratory cultures, it has the potential for reducing the Mexican bean beetle to a minor pest requiring few or no sprays.

Each Orius bug destroys 20 or more flower thrips per day. He and his fellows are responsible for reducing high spring populations of this insect to low levels for the remainder of the season.

Our native ladybird beetles, that come into our gardens in late spring, lay their orange-yellow eggs among aphids on flowers and vegetables where each alligator-like larva sucks the juices from 10 to 20 aphids per day for a total of 300 or more during its growth period. Thus, thriving aphid colonies developing in early spring, virtually disappear for the summer and do not reappear until autumn when temperatures are lower, and the ladybird beetles are less active.

In contrast to these recognized but highly efficient parasites and predators discussed above, much attention is given by amateur ecologists in their publications to the more conspicuous but least effective predators. They urge you to buy preying mantid egg masses and pints of ladybird beetles and release them in your garden for season-long insect control. You should realize that the preying mantids hatch from the egg masses in late spring. The tiny mantids scramble for safety — usually into dense shrubbery — to avoid being eaten by their brothers and sisters. Of the hundreds that hatch in the spring, only a few survive until fall and they are usually found in the shrub border, rarely on the more exposed vegetables where you need them.

One authority has stated that "the chief benefit to be derived from the purchase of mantid egg masses is the feeling of virtue in believing that you have established a highly beneficial insect which will protect the neighborhood by destroying many harmful garden pests. Of the hundreds of young mantids that come tumbling out of a case, perchance a few will survive. With avid appetites and rapacious front legs they capture many insects; including their brothers and sisters, and harmful insects as well as beneficial insects. Nevertheless, the mantid is a handsome insect that is interesting to have around. So let us continue to protect it and encourage others to do the same, but do not depend upon it to rid our garden of all noxious pests."

The ladybird beetles you buy are collected from their hibernating quarters in California canyons and are shipped to you. When you release them in your garden they usually disperse to other areas just as they disperse from their hibernating quarters in canyons or woodlands — often for several miles — in search of cultivated fields. Few, if any, remain for long in your garden. Ladybird beetles found in your garden are local, naturally occurring beetles which migrate from hibernating sources early in the spring.

Basic Fertilizer Practices

The average home gardener grows perhaps 30 to 40 different types of plants and trees. Out of that total number, only a few need really personalized care. The rest will grow very satisfactorily with a minimum of attention from the gardener if—and this is a big "if"—the basic requirements for a plant to grow have been satisfied from the beginning.

Nutrients in the soil are a basic requirement of all plants. Here we describe the general methods of applying these nutrients in different forms of fertilizer to three general groups of plants: vegetables, lawn grasses and trees. Plants within these groups and others that demand special attention can be found in Special Handling, page 84 on.

When it comes time to fertilize, the gardener may begin to doubt just how simple the process really is—the number of different forms and formulations of today's fertilizer products can be bewildering. The information on pages 64 and 65 will help you decide which form—dry, liquid, slow-release or other—is best for the different groups of plants.

Relative need for nutrients

The following suggestions about groups of garden plants are given as general guides. Gardeners should be aware that individual species within these groups vary considerably. After each group of plants, the need for the primary nutrients—nitrogen, phosphorus and potassium—is indicated as high, medium or low.

Vegetables .... High
Herbs............ Medium to low
Lawns .... Medium to high
Fruits .... Medium
Annual flowers .... Medium
Perennial flowers . Medium to low
Deciduous shrubs . Medium to low
Evergreen shrubs .... Low
Deciduous shade
trees .... Medium to low
Evergreen shade. trees .... Low

When to fertilize

The general rule to remember about timing nitrogen fertilizer applications is that they are necessary *when* a plant is growing, not *to make* a plant grow. Upsetting the natural rhythm of growth can result in injury to the plant.

Nitrogen is the nutrient most responsible for stimulating vegetative growth. Applying a fertilizer containing nitrogen to a dormant plant can cause it to leaf out before the time is right. Plants out-of-doors are most seriously affected: new leaf tissue is particularly cold-sensitive, or tender, so an untimely feeding could result in frost- or cold-damaged plants.

There are several fertilizer formulations which do not contain nitrogen, the most popular of which is 0-10-10. A fertilizer with this formulation can be safely used during the non-growing season, and is often applied to citrus, azaleas, cymbidium orchids, and other plants to promote healthy flowering and fruiting.

Fertilizing Vegetables

Recommendations for fertilizing vegetables are usually given in the following words: "Apply 3 to 4 pounds of a 5-10-10 fertilizer per 100 square feet of garden space." All that is well and good, as long as you are using a 5-10-10 formula. If the fertilizer you want to use has a different formula—say, one with a higher nitrogen

Drop spreaders are the most popular way to apply dry fertilizer to average sized lawns. These spreaders are fast, easy-to-use, and accurate.

You can broadcast dry fertilizers by hand, but the results are sometimes uneven — when applying fertilizers by hand apply in a criss-cross pattern to reduce spottiness.

For applying liquid fertilizers to lawns, gardens, and for foliar-feeding, a hose-end sprayer is an indispensible garden tool. Several models are available.

content as indicated by the first number in the formula—the rate of application should be reduced to avoid nitrogen burn. A high phosphorus fertilizer such as 6-18-6 is often recommended for vegetables as a starter food.

In the following chart you see how the amount to be applied decreases as the percentage of nitrogen increases (the percentage of nitrogen is indicated by the first number in each series):

Formula	Pounds per 100 square feet
5-10-10	3.5
6-18-6	2.8
8-24-8	2.0
12-6-6	1.4
16-16-16	1.0

If you are using a liquid fertilizer, it is easy to convert the recommendations made for dry fertilizer into pints or cups: a pint of dry fertilizer weighs about 1 pound; a cup about ½ pound.

Ways to apply dry fertilizers:

(1) Mix with the soil before planting. Spread fertilizer evenly over soil at the rate called for on the fertilizer bag or box, and work it into the soil with a spade or power tiller.

(2) Apply narrow bands of fertilizer in furrows 2 to 3 inches from the seed and 1 to 2 inches deeper than the seeds or plants are to be placed (see illustration). Careless placement of the fertilizer band too close to the seeds will burn the roots of the seedlings. The best technique is to stretch a string where the seed row is to be planted. With a corner of a hoe, dig a furrow 3 inches deep, 3 inches to one side of, and parallel to the string. Spread the fertilizer in the furrow and cover with soil. Repeat the banding operation on the other side of the string. Then sow seeds underneath the string.

For plants widely spaced, such as tomatoes, fertilizers can be placed in bands 6 inches long for each plant or in a circle around the plant. Make the bands 4 inches from the plant base. Or, in the planting hole, place the fertilizer at the bottom of the hole, work it in the soil, place a layer of soil about 2 inches deep over the fertilized soil and then put the plant in the hole.

(3) Apply dry fertilizer as a side-dressing after plants are up and growing. Scatter fertilizer on both sides of the row 6 to 8 inches from the plants. Rake it into the soil and water thoroughly.

Banding is one way to satisfy the need of many plants, especially tomatoes, for phosphorus as the first roots develop. When fertilizers are broadcast and worked into soil, much of the phosphorus is locked up by the soil and is not immediately available to the plant. By concentrating the phosphorus in the band, you give the plant what it needs even though much of the phosphorus stays locked up.

Another way to satisfy the need for phosphorus is to use a starter solution when setting out transplants of tomatoes, eggplant, peppers or cabbage. Any liquid fertilizer high in phosphorus can be used as a starter solution. Follow directions on the label.

Or you can make your own starter solution with the dry fertilizer you are using if it is high in phosphorus. When using a 5-10-10 formulation, dissolve 1 pound in 5 gallons of water. Don't expect it to dissolve completely; stir it occasionally as you apply it. Place the transplant in the planting hole, fill the hole half full of soil, pour in a cupful of the solution and finish filling the hole with soil.

A specialized root feeder for trees and large shrubs applies nutrients directly in the root zone. If the soil is compacted, the process can be a lengthy one.

Proportioners come in many models, but all work on the same principle: they add liquid fertilizer concentrations to irrigation water at a pre-set rate.

For large areas, it is hard to beat a broadcast spreader. They are available in hand-held and push-type models, and are very fast and efficient.

Trees

Measuring a tree trunk diameter with calipers.

Feeding a young tree with a Root Feeder.

Spraying a needled evergreen with a hose-end sprayer.

Fertilizing Lawns

There are four basic methods of applying fertilizers to lawns:

Broadcasting. You can broadcast dry pelleted fertilizer by hand, but it requires an experienced hand to achieve an efficient, even application. Use this method only in very small areas or if there is no other alternative available to you. The most even hand coverage can be had using the "checkerboard" method: apply one-half of the total amount of fertilizer by walking in rows in one direction, and apply the remaining portion by walking perpendicular to the original rows.

Hose-end sprayers. Liquid fertilizers are applied by hand with a sprayer attached to the hose. Read the directions on both the fertilizer label and the sprayer carefully. The rates are set according to the ratio of liquid fertilizer and water mixed in the sprayer jar. Also, make sure all parts of the sprayer are attached and in good working order, or you may unwittingly water the lawn rather than fertilize it.

Drop spreaders are the most popular method of applying dry fertilizer to lawns. They require more passes than a broadcast spreader but are useful for smaller lawns. When using a drop spreader, overlap the wheels enough so no strips are left underfed; otherwise your lawn will show uneven greening in a few days. But don't overlap too much, especially on turns, or you will burn the lawn.

The best technique for applying lawn food with a drop-type spreader is shown in the illustrations on page 98. Cover the ends first. Then go back and forth the long way. To avoid double applications, gradually shut off the spreader as you approach the end strips. Keep the spreader closed while you are turning around, backing up or stopped. For even and thorough coverage, walk at normal speed and keep the spreader level. For best coverage, follow the manufacturer's directions and the label on the fertilizer bag.

If you happen to spill or drop extra dry fertilizer in one area, brush or vacuum it up and then completely soak the area with water to avoid burning.

After fertilizing, brush or wash out the spreader and dry thoroughly before storing.

A broadcast spreader is probably the easiest way to apply dry fertilizer to a lawn. There are hand-held and push-wheeled models. Both models throw the fertilizer pellets over a wide swath by means of a whirling wheel at the base of the hopper. They are easier to use than drop spreaders, especially on large lawns, because they require fewer passes for the same area of lawn. Make sure you know how wide a swath the spreader throws so you can tell how far apart to space your passes, and try not to apply in windy weather.

Fertilizing Trees

Nitrogen is the element to which most established trees generally respond. Young trees may need a complete fertilizer for establishment. They grow more rapidly following fertilization, more quickly reaching landscape size. However, mature trees usually need little or no fertilization as long as they have good leaf color and grow reasonably well. In fact, increased vigor may needlessly increase the size of trees and the density of the leaves. Then, the leaves on the inside of the trees or the plants under them grow poorly because of heavy shade. (Note: Because fruit trees are carefully pruned, this situation does not apply, and fertilization is considered an essential management tool for a good fruit harvest.)

As a starter, apply at a rate of 2 to 4 pounds of actual nitrogen per 1,000 square feet. If you do not want to use a simple nitrogen fertilizer (ammonium nitrate, ammonium sulfate, calcium nitrate or urea), a "complete" fertilizer is fine. Read directions and adjust the amount according to the percentage of nitrogen in the particular fertilizer. If it's 12 percent, as in 12-6-6, use 8½ pounds to equal one pound of nitrogen.

Another way to figure how much to apply is to measure the diameter of the tree trunk. For trees over 6 inches in diameter use 2 to 4 pounds of a fertilizer that contains 12 percent nitrogen (such as 12-6-6) for each inch of diameter. For smaller trees, use 1 to 2 pounds of 12 percent nitrogen fertilizer for each inch of diameter.

Because nitrogen is transient, use the necessary amount in two applications. One-half in spring and the other half in summer is a good program. Keep the fertilizer at least 12 inches away from the trunk to avoid injuring it. After the first year, apply nitrogen fertilizer to an area having a radius of one and a quarter times that of the tree canopy. After application, sprinkle-irrigate the area thoroughly to wash the fertilizer into the soil. This begins conversion of the less soluble forms of nitrogen, and avoids burning the grass if the tree is planted in a lawn.

Let the trees be your guide as to the amount to apply. If growth is excessive on young trees, put on less next time, or skip a year. If shoot growth is shorter than you want and leaf color pale, double the rate. As trees mature, fertilize only if growth or leaf color is not up to expectation.

If a tree isn't responding to nitrogen, describe its symptoms to your nursery or county extension agent.

Most trees grow satisfactorily over a wide range of soils and soil pH. Well-drained soils in high-rainfall areas usually are acid, while those in areas of low rainfall are usually neutral or alkaline. In some alkaline soils a number of trees may be low in iron, as evidenced by their pale yellow leaves with fine, darker green veins. These symptoms are most obvious on the first growth during spring. An acid-forming nitrogen fertilizer, such as ammonium sulfate, may help. If the symptoms are severe, soil sulfur can be worked into the surface soil at about 10 to 20 pounds per 1,000 square feet. The use of iron chelates for correction of chlorosis brings quicker and more certain action, although the correction may last only one or two seasons. Apply chelates as directed on the label. In areas having alkaline soil, you may want to avoid species most likely to show iron deficiency.

Foliar feeding—emergency treatment

Foliar feeding is used when (1) insufficient fertilizer was used before planting, (2) a quick growth response is wanted, (3) micronutrients such as iron or zinc are locked in the soil, or (4) the soil is too cold for conversion of nutrient elements into usable forms.

Foliar-applied nutrients are absorbed and used by the plant quite rapidly. Absorption begins within minutes after application and with most nutrients it is completed within 1 to 2 days.

Foliar nutrition is a supplement to soil nutrition, not a substitute; but it can be a supplement at a critical time for the plant. At transplanting time, an application of phosphorus spray will help in the establishment of the young plant.

For perennial plants, early spring growth is usually limited by cold soil, even when the air is warm. Under such conditions, soil microorganisms are not active to convert nutrients into forms available for roots to absorb. Yet, if the nutrients were available, the plant could grow. A nutrient spray to the foliage will provide the needed nutrients immediately to the plants, allowing the plant to begin growth before the roots are able to absorb nutrients from the soil.

Newly transplanted plants may benefit from foliar sprays. Until new roots are formed, the plant is completely dependent upon stored nutrients to maintain itself. When these stored nutrients are used up or are deficient, the ability of the plant to become established is greatly reduced. Foliar nutrient sprays may alleviate this problem.

Proportioners. There are many different types of fertilizer proportioners, all of which perform a similar function: they all add concentrated liquid fertilizer to irrigation water at a specific rate, predetermined by the proportioner itself. Common hose-end sprayers are one type; nurseries also offer small brass units which can be attached in between the hose and the faucet, with a separate small hose which draws the liquid concentrated fertilizer directly from your own container. Models range from a few to several hundred dollars.

Vegetables

Fertilizer banding when planting seeds.

1" 2" to 3"

Side dressing fertilizer on established plants.

When transplanting, firm the soil around the rootball, water to settle the soil . . .

Fill any settled area with more soil mix.

Water

Chances are about 9 to 1 that if you show a plant
—be it shrub, tree, herb, flower or vegetable—
to a plant doctor, the diagnosis will be "too much
water," "too little water" or "bad watering habits."
Here's what you can do about it.

Watering isn't difficult to do properly, and it's easy to give gardeners general advice on the subject, but offering specific advice in a general way is downright impossible. Even advisors with the best intentions often end up offering muddled instructions when they try to combine the specific with the general.

General advice on when and how to water a specific site is difficult because there are so many variables to be considered: soil type and slope, humidity, type of plant grown, weather, season, light intensity, wind, temperature, whether the soil is covered with a mulch, and on and on.

All these factors are best known to the individual gardener and so the first word of advice to you, the gardener, should be: "Know your garden"—the characteristics of the soil and plants, and how the location of the garden affects your watering, etc. With this personal knowledge, you can develop an art of watering that transcends technical advice.

Water and Soil Character

It's impossible to talk about watering without talking about the characteristics of the soil being watered. The characteristics of your own soil are the single most important factor influencing your watering practices. If you've improved your soil to the point where it has the

Concentrating water in the root zone of the plant is the objective of many forms of irrigation. Here, a gardener has cut both ends from a coffee can and submerged it next to a squash plant. The can is filled several times—water run-off and waste is greatly reduced.

characteristics of a "made loam," more than half the watering battle is already won. Most plants grown in a good loam soil are far more tolerant of a range of watering practices, good and bad, than if they are in either clayey or sandy soils, both of which are notoriously difficult to water properly. This isn't to say that you can't learn to handle a clay or sand soil successfully—many gardeners have —but it's a challenging procedure involving much trial and error.

The ideal garden soil admits nearly all the water that falls on it, holds a large quantity within the fine pores, allows any excess to drain away and is protected by surface mulches from excessive evaporation.

It is harder to establish proper water-air-plant relationships in a clay soil because water enters the small soil pores slowly; overwatering causes flooding which deprives plant roots of oxygen and the soil becomes easily compacted.

The gardener who manages a clay soil must learn to provide alternate wetting and partial drying of the soil. The drying will allow air into the soil.

Sandy soils provide fast drainage and good aeration, but fail in the water-holding department.

Generally speaking, the coarser the particles that make up a soil, the less water the soil will hold. Sandy soils (they have the coarsest particles) hold only about ¼ inch of water per foot of depth. Sandy loams commonly hold about ¾ inch of water per foot; fine sandy loams, about 1¼ inches; and silt loams, clay loams and clays, about 2½ to 3 inches. Although these are rough figures, they clearly show that different soil types demand different watering schedules.

The addition of organic matter to any of the soil types mentioned above will have the effect of equalizing their water requirements. Large amounts of organic matter may increase the water-holding capacity of the sandy soils, and "open up" heavier silt loams and clay soils to allow more air and water to enter.

Testing capacity and drainage

If there is one justification for saying "I just haven't got a green thumb," it's in the watering of plants in problem soils (the soils most gardeners have). It takes time to know the watering needs of each plant and to water deeply or shallowly, frequently or infrequently, plant by plant. And then to have to know about the soil-water characteristics in the garden makes the job even more complicated.

There are several ways you can determine a soil's ability to hold both moisture and air. A series of tests with pots or cans (see illustration) will give you good answers to questions about water retention and soil aeration.

To test your soil's **water-holding capacity,** first allow the soil samples to dry. Then fill the pots uniformly, without tamping the

A severely wilted piggyback plant (*Tolmiea menziesii*) shows its dramatic powers of recovery when water is applied. The process took less than three hours.

soil down, to within about an inch of the top. Pour in a pint of water. Then note how long it takes the water to begin to drip into the jars below and how much water comes from each sample. Compare the water retention capacity of soils from different parts of your yard by comparing the amounts of water left in the soil—the amounts that haven't dripped through—after the dripping has stopped.

To test the soil's **capacity for drainage,** you must wait until the container has just stopped dripping. The soil is then completely saturated—it's holding as much water as it can. Now pour another pint of water into the container and notice the time it takes the full pint of water to move through the soil and collect in the jar beneath the soil container.

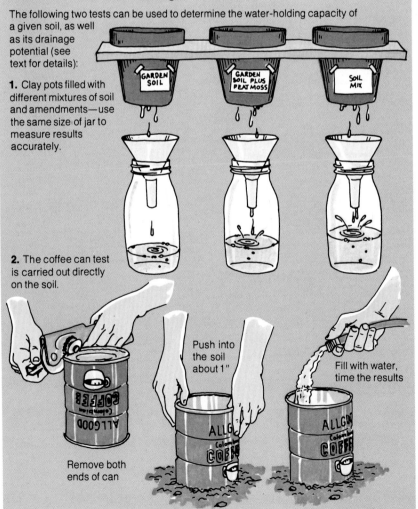

Water retention and drainage

The following two tests can be used to determine the water-holding capacity of a given soil, as well as its drainage potential (see text for details):

1. Clay pots filled with different mixtures of soil and amendments—use the same size of jar to measure results accurately.

GARDEN SOIL

GARDEN SOIL PLUS PEAT MOSS

SOIL MIX

2. The coffee can test is carried out directly on the soil.

Remove both ends of can

Push into the soil about 1"

Fill with water, time the results

Soil structure

Compacted Soil: The particles are packed close together with little space left for air or water.

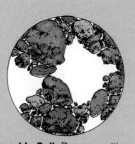

Crumbly Soil: Decomposition of organic matter helps aggregate dry particles into porous crumbs.

Saturated Soil: If about half the water from rain or irrigation does not drain through the soil, plants may drown.

Moist Soil: A film of water between soil particles, and air in all but the small pores, means soil is well drained.

Another method of checking the water infiltration rate and the drainage, which some gardeners claim is more accurate than the previous test, uses a coffee can with both ends removed. In the area you want to test, push the can into the soil to a depth of 1 inch. Fill the can with water and watch to see how long it takes to disappear. Test the soil's drainage capability by filling the can again and noting the length of time it takes to drain through.

How can you tell which test result is good and which is bad? One way is to compare your soil with one of the synthetic "loams" represented by the U.C. (University of California) mix in the West and the Cornell mix in the East (see page 40). These are predictably fast-draining soils with good water-retaining characteristics.

Other interesting tests can be carried out with this same equipment: Mix organic matter (peat moss, ground bark or similar material) with a batch of your garden soil and test against untreated soil.

With any glass container, you can see why adding gravel or a quantity of broken pottery to the bottom of the pot does not improve drainage in containers (contrary to what many gardeners may have told you). Gravel in the

bottom of the container does the same thing as the bottom of the pot itself—it breaks the blotter action of the soil as the water moves down through it. Gravel, sand, organic matter, or any material with a drastically different texture impairs good drainage. To prevent soil from being washed out of the pot as water drains through, place just *one* curved piece of broken pottery, copper or plastic screening, or a bottle cap over the drainage hole.

Note: In all drainage tests, the first few waterings will not give true results. Repeat the waterings until the soils are settled evenly.

If you have a fairly **shallow topsoil** with a layer of hardpan underneath it, you'll have to watch your watering habits closely. Such soils may look all right on the surface, but the hardpan layer keeps roots from developing fully and keeps water confined to the top layer of soil.

The small amounts of water that can be held by the shallow topsoil layer is rapidly depleted in hot dry weather, and the plants will show signs of wilt soon after watering.

Under such conditions, water should be applied in moderate to small amounts and frequently—much the same way you apply

water to plants in containers. Heavy watering may virtually "drown" the plants by overfilling the soil pores and eliminating oxygen from the root zone. (If you want to plant deep-rooted trees, shrubs or perennials in a shallow soil, see illustration, page 82.)

How Important is Water?

Applying water correctly is one of the best forms of insurance for success a gardener can have. Don't forget, though, that the best watering practices in the world will not make up for deficiencies of mineral nutrients, lack of weed control, or the variety's lack of adaptability to your climate. There is little point in supplying water to plants that are unable to make productive use of it because of poor soil or poor soil management.

Amount and Timing

While it is difficult to give general advice on specific watering practices, a couple of time-honored rules should be followed. The first concerns the amount of water to apply at any one time, and the rule is simple: fill the root zone, then allow the soil to dry out somewhat before the next watering.

If you water thoroughly and too frequently, there's a good chance that you'll cut off the supply of air in the soil by filling all of the air spaces with water. Then root growth stops, and the longer the air is cut off, the greater the root damage. Damaged roots can be invaded by rot-causing microorganisms in the soil, and the plant can be easily killed by root rot.

On the other hand, if you water too lightly and frequently, the water never has a chance to move very far into the soil. Plant roots grow only in areas where there are moisture, nutrients and air. The soil surrounding the roots may be nutrient-rich and contain plenty of air, but without moisture, roots will not grow there. The result of shallow watering is shallow-rooted plants. If you miss a couple of waterings, a shallow-rooted plant does not tap reserves of water deeper in the soil. Consequently, the plant cannot survive even brief periods of drought or high temperatures.

The general rule-of-thumb would go like this: When you

Some gardeners find that an oscillating sprinkler set in the middle of a garden works satisfactorily. Others complain of muddy walkways and weed problems.

One way to measure the amount of water applied to a lawn is to set out same-sized containers on a grid pattern in the area covered by the sprinkler. Check the amount of water in the containers at thirty minute intervals. The amount of water individual lawns need varies, but the general rule of thumb is to apply one inch of water with each irrigation.

water, water well and learn how long it takes for your particular soil to dry slightly between waterings.

One of the general questions about watering is, "When is the best time to water?" There are plenty of local prejudices and differing schools of thought on this subject, but commonsense may be the best advice of all. You can reduce plant diseases and lose less water to evaporation by watering in the early morning. The reasoning behind this is clear: leaves (including blades of grass) that stay damp through the night invite attack by disease-causing organisms. By watering them in the morning hours, you give plants a chance to dry off before nightfall.

How much is enough?

This question requires several answers. Lawns, shallow-rooted annual flowers and vegetables, mature trees and shrubs, container-grown plants, and other plants in various stages of growth all have different water needs, and the climate has a lot to do with it: how hot it is, how humid, how many sunny or cloudy days, etc. But if you remember the general advice—to water thoroughly when you do water—you'll have few water-related problems.

How can you tell if you're watering thoroughly? The best way is to take a look underground, past the top 3 or 4 inches of soil, using a shovel or trowel. Check to make sure the water is moving through this top layer and into the soil below, where the roots need to grow.

Lawns should be watered when the soil begins to dry out, before the grass actually wilts. At that stage, areas of the lawn will begin to change color, picking up a blue-green or smoky tinge. An even more evident signal is a loss of resilience—footprints will make a long-lasting imprint rather than bouncing right back.

Several areas of the country have been affected by serious drought conditions over the past few years. During such times, lawns are hardest hit for lack of water. The University of California recommends the following practices when water use is restricted:

(1) Do not apply fertilizer to lawns until the rains return.

(2) Mow your grass higher and less often. Don't let it grow more than twice the recommended mowing height, however.

(3) Reduce competition for water by eliminating weeds from the lawn.

(4) Irrigate without runoff to root zone depth (about 6 inches) when your lawn shows the need.

These are not normal lawn care practices—it is survival irrigation, so don't be surprised if the lawn develops a spotty, thinned appearance. The lawn will recover with normal weather conditions and good lawn care practices.

Tensiometers can generally take the place of a shovel or trowel, and several inexpensive and uncomplicated models have appeared in the past few years. You can tell a great deal about what's going on beneath the top layers of soil in various parts of the garden in a few minutes.

A tensiometer is basically a long, thin metal probe with a small meter (much like a light meter) mounted on the top. When the probe is stuck in the soil, the amount of moisture at its tip (often made of ceramic material) registers on the meter. The results can be surprising: soil that looks dry on the surface can be quite damp 8 inches underground, and vice versa. Tensiometers are also helpful if you're growing plants in containers, either indoors or out.

Using a tensiometer is a simple operation. The probe should be inserted 12 to 24 inches deep under shrubs and 24 to 36 inches deep under trees. If the meter reads in the 50 to 70 centibar range (moderately dry), apply irrigation water as you would normally. Check the moisture readings again, at the same depth, 12 to 24 hours after watering. If the reading is 5 to 15 centibars, you have applied the right amount of water. If the reading is less than 5, apply less water next time; if more than 15, apply more water.

Hand-watering—the delights and dilemmas.

Nothing we say here will convince ardent hand-waterers and dust-settlers to stop what they've been doing forever. And we're not denying the fact that to be in the garden at the end of a long summer's day, with hose in hand spraying everything in sight, is unquestionably one of life's considerable pleasures. So we'll leave it at this: shallow watering usually does more harm than good. So if you're a compulsive end-of-the-day water-sprayer, make sure that isn't the only watering your garden gets.

While on the subject of hand-watering, let's face the controversy over whether or not to spray plants lightly during a hot spell. In periods of extended heat, many plants wilt around the middle of the day. Basically, the leaf surface becomes hot enough that the plant sends a signal to the leaves that makes them shut down transpiration, their natural cooling operation, and the leaves begin to wilt. Many gardeners come to the rescue by hurriedly spraying the leaves with cool water. And an equal number say that such an activity causes leaves to burn—that the water creates a lens effect which focuses light rays and causes burns.

We're in favor of the gardener who sprays water during a hot spell. A light shower does indeed cool the leaf surface, and dehydration can be avoided to some extent. We have yet to see a case of leaves being burned by the light application of clear water.

Different kinds of water

Generally speaking, if you can drink the water where you live, it is safe for plants. How you use water is far more important to plants than its chemical content. One thing to beware of, though, is softened water.

Softened water. Water softeners of the zeolite type produce water that can injure plants, especially indoor plants in containers. The zeolite softener replaces the calcium in water (the element that makes water "hard") with sodium. This sodium does not settle out or evaporate; in fact, it accumulates in container and outdoor soils alike. Long-term use of such water can cause soils to become much less permeable and can cause leaves of sodium-sensitive plants (such as citrus, avocado and orchids) to burn. If you have a water softener, install a tap in the water line before it gets to the softener, so that you'll have un-

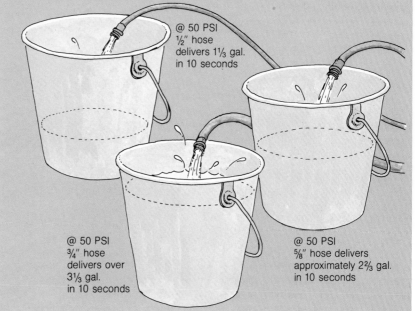

Garden hoses

A hose can be a gardener's best friend or a worst enemy. A hose of poor quality causes more headaches than it's worth.

A well-made hose will be flexible in any weather. This is usually the case with high grade rubber and laminated filament hoses. The hose should be long enough to reach all areas of your yard, and have a large enough diameter to supply sufficient quantities of water. The larger the diameter of the hose, the more water it can deliver. Home garden variety hoses are available in ¾ inch, ⅝ inch and ½ inch diameters. The ⅝ inch is a usual choice for a medium-size home lawn area.

@ 50 PSI
½" hose delivers 1⅓ gal. in 10 seconds

@ 50 PSI
⅝" hose delivers approximately 2⅔ gal. in 10 seconds

@ 50 PSI
¾" hose delivers over 3⅓ gal. in 10 seconds

Water in the garden isn't always serious business. Where there's a sprinkler, a lawn, and a hot day, there's fun to be had.

softened water for your plants. Or follow the advice of the Cooperative Extension of the University of California.

"Softened water can be treated to eliminate these hazards. The treatment involves simply adding calcium that was present before softening removed it. This can nullify the effect of the sodium added in the softening process.

"Gypsum (calcium sulfate), available at most nurseries, is a cheap and safe material to use for this purpose. Its safety feature is its relatively low solubility, yet enough gypsum can be dissolved to treat softened waters effectively. One-half level teaspoon per gallon of softened water should be sufficient in most cases to supply the necessary calcium and change softened water to an unsoftened state, thereby eliminating the risk of its use."

Gray water. In some areas, extended periods of drought during the past few years forced people to use "gray" water in their gardens. Like softened water, gray water—water from the rinse cycle of dish and clothes washers or from bathroom tubs and basins—has a high sodium content from the soap used in washing.

Gardeners concerned about

this additional sodium and its effect on the soil and plants found that the addition of gypsum directly to the soil maintained the good soil structure that long-term applications of high-sodium water would tend to destroy. Follow manufacturer's instructions concerning the amounts to apply.

Hard water. In areas where soil is very alkaline and the water is hard, it is difficult to grow acid-loving plants. The generous use of peat moss and fertilizers that are acid in reaction (see page 26) will help offset the alkaline soil and water. Plants such as azaleas, gardenias and camellias will benefit from regular applications of an iron chelate (see page 52) to keep the foliage a healthy dark green. When new foliage of these plants is yellow, use a solution of 1 ounce iron sulfate in 2 gallons of water. Repeat this watering every two weeks until new growth has a normal color.

Distilled water. Using distilled water (water which has had all salts and other solids removed) may seem like an extreme practice for the garden, but there are times when it is beneficial. Because of the limited amount of soil used in growing bonsai and mame bonsai, specialists find

distilled water beneficial in preventing salt build-up in the soil and on unglazed pots. Instead of using the commercially available distilled water, which is relatively expensive, many gardeners who worry about salt build-up have large barrels to collect rain water. Rain water, through the process of evaporation, is naturally distilled.

Wetting agents. If you've ever had trouble getting peat moss, ground bark, or other organic matter to absorb water, you should investigate wetting agents. There are several commercial formulations, both liquid and dry, which make water "wetter." A dramatic example of their effect can be seen by filling a glass with water so that the water level is actually above the top of the glass. Unless jarred, the surface tension of the water will keep the water from dribbling out. Add a drop of wetting agent, which reduces the surface tension, and the water will immediately drain over the top.

Wetting agents in the dry form can be mixed right into a synthetic soil mix to make initial waterings easier. The liquid form can be put in a hose-end sprayer and used to get water to penetrate lawns with thatch buildup. The liquid form can also be mixed in a watering can and used to thoroughly wet hanging baskets, pots and other containers.

Hydroponics

A chapter on water would not be complete without mentioning the most extreme form of water in the garden: hydroponics.

Hydroponics, simply defined, is the growing of plants in a liquid containing nutrients rather than soil. In the garden, plants are anchored in the soil and draw water and nutrients from it. In hydroponics, a water solution rich with the necessary nutrients is washed or pumped through a mix of light gravel, fiberglass, or other inert medium that anchors the plants.

Unfortunately, space does not permit a full discussion of the various methods of hydroponic gardening here. If you are interested in the subject, another book in the Ortho Book Series, *How To Build & Use Greenhouses,* has a complete and informative section on hydroponics.

Methods of Applying Water

Over the years gardeners and farmers have developed many ways of applying water to plants. On the next three pages we illustrate some of the newest and oldest methods and describe the benefits and drawbacks of each. It's up to you to decide which is best for your particular garden. But whatever method you choose, keep in mind this general advice:

If you have shallow topsoil on top of hardpan, water lightly and frequently.

Otherwise, water thoroughly and let the soil dry out somewhat before the next watering.

Water early enough in the day that the leaves are dry by night-time.

In really hot and dry weather, don't be afraid to give the leaves of outdoor plants a cool shower.

Don't use zeolite-softened water; do add gypsum to the soil if you want to use gray water.

When irrigating clay or similar "tight" soils, apply water over short periods, separated by a soaking-in period of at least twice the length of the application time—for example, 10 minutes on, 20 min-

utes off, 10 minutes on. For clay soils, use a sprinkler that emits water at as slow a rate as possible.

Treat steep slopes as you would a clay soil, to minimize runoff.

When irrigating sandy loams or other open soils, apply water in one continuous period.

The best time to water is early morning when the sun and wind are both low.

If you have the choice, water on the cooler days during the summer.

Set sprinklers to avoid waste on sidewalks and driveways.

Keep sprinkler heads clean to assure even distribution of water.

Flooding

Flooding is most often used in areas with extreme summer heat. Lawns and some vegetables and fruit trees can be flooded over a large area to ensure complete saturation. Not practical for small areas, or in areas where walkways are necessary.

Furrow irrigation

Furrow irrigation is probably the most common method of vegetable and berry watering. The advantages are in keeping the irrigation water confined to the root zone of the plants, and in inhibiting weed growth in unwatered areas. Furrows can be placed to allow dry walkways between paths.

Soakers

Soakers can emit water slowly and economically. They do not disturb the soil structure and do not cause the crust formation common with overhead sprinklers. Many gardeners leave soakers in location from one season to the next.

Underground sprinkler systems

Underground sprinkler systems are very convenient for large gardens with expanses of lawn. Good, even coverage is achieved with a minimum of guesswork. Can be installed on a timer for further convenience and regularity.

Hose-end sprinklers

Hose-end sprinklers come in many shapes and sizes to match the wide variety of irrigation needs. Because of their limited range, they are less convenient than a permanent sprinkler system, but also much less expensive. To avoid wasting water, choose the sprinkler best suited to the area watered.

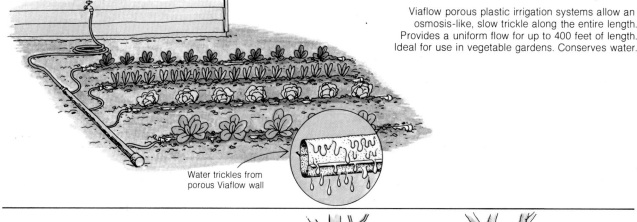

Porous wall systems

Viaflow porous plastic irrigation systems allow an osmosis-like, slow trickle along the entire length. Provides a uniform flow for up to 400 feet of length. Ideal for use in vegetable gardens. Conserves water.

Water trickles from porous Viaflow wall

Drip/trickle systems

Several drip/trickle systems are available to the home gardener. Different nozzles are available for different growing situations. Most provide small, steady and precise amounts of water exactly where needed. Most require a filtration unit to avoid clogging.

Stick-in sprayer with adjustable spray arc

Water-loops in various sizes water the area surrounding each plant.

Drip irrigation

Drip irrigation hardware permits many types of watering systems for container plants. Here a length of plastic pipe with a half dozen spaghetti tubes with drip spitters attached delivers water in the small amount the containers hold. It's a good way to "vacationize" your garden.

Hose-end nozzles

New and old watering devices can make clean-up and watering chores easier on the gardener. There's virtually a hose-end nozzle for every need.

Misters and foggers

Mist spray nozzles give many container plants the fog they need on dry hot days.

Extender

The watering stick—a water breaker—will deliver a high volume of water without disturbing the soil.

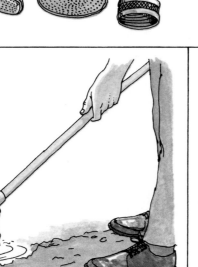

Hanging basket watering

The shepherd's watering extension makes the watering of hanging baskets a simple job with no dribbling down the arm.

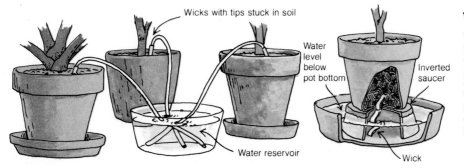

Wicks with tips stuck in soil

Water level below pot bottom

Inverted saucer

Water reservoir

Wick

Water wicks

Wick watering can be arranged to take care of watering needs for a week or more. Wicks running from a pail of water to the soil of containers will give a continuous supply of water. We use wicks of glass wool and fray the ends that go in the soil. Special wicks are available. A nylon clothesline will also serve as a wick.

Planting procedures

It's disappointing to buy a healthy plant, tree or shrub in a nursery, only to have it diminish in strength and beauty after it's been planted in your own garden. One of the best ways to avoid the problem is by following the appropriate planting procedure illustrated on these pages.

But sometimes the trouble has started even before you get to the planting step. The following are a few good gardening don'ts:

Don't have the can cut at the nursery unless you are going to plant the shrub or tree right away. Anything in a can that has been cut is almost impossible to water properly for any length of time.

Don't pick a container plant up by the trunk or stem—the roots may not be well established.

If a plant won't come out of a metal can easily at planting time, *cut* the can with a pair of tin snips or can cutters—don't knock the can about trying to get the plant out.

Don't take any plant out of its container before you've dug the hole. And don't leave a bare-root tree's roots exposed: it takes no time at all for the sun and wind to dry out the all-important root hairs that cover the larger roots. If you have a series of bare-root trees or shrubs to plant, cover them with moist burlap or sawdust until the holes are ready.

Don't put a layer of organic matter into the bottom of a planting hole. Many gardeners dig a hole for a tree or shrub, and put a layer of organic matter or a layer of soil which is quite different from the surrounding soil into the bottom of the hole, thinking that it encourages new roots and makes it easier for them to get started. This is not so. The best practice is to make a transitional soil mixture to backfill around a newly planted tree or shrub. This transitional mixture should be a combination of 50 percent of the native soil and 50 percent of the soil in which the plant is already growing. For example: a gardener wants to plant a balled and burlapped conifer which has been grown in a sandy soil into a garden which has predominately clay soil. The backfill around the tree should consist of 50 percent sand and 50 percent of the native clay soil.

After you've planted a tree or shrub, it may take only a day or two for wind and sun to pull water out of its rootball even when the surrounding soil is wet. Make sure that the rootball stays moist while the roots are spreading out beyond it. To do this build a temporary basin a little larger than the rootball was inside the permanent basin. Water every other day for the first 10 days in hot weather.

Planting hole

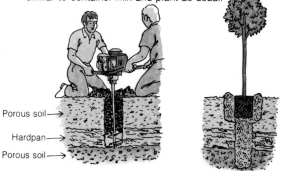

Slightly above grade

Width: Dig the hole twice the rootball diameter or large enough to accommodate bareroots.

Depth: In clay soil, dig 1 to 2 inches less than the depth of the rootball or original soil line. In sandy soil or loam, the original soil level should be at or slightly higher than the garden soil.

Be sure bottom soil has settled, sides are straight up and down, roughened-up for easy root penetration, and the bottom is flat or slightly raised in the center.

Check planting depth

After watering to settle the soil, check to be certain the original soil line is at the proper level. If it's too low—

Bareroot: Grasp the trunk near the soil and lift an inch or so higher than the proper level and let it settle back.

Balled in Burlap or Containers: Carefully place a shovel beneath the rootball and pry up while lifting on the trunk. Raise it an inch or two above the proper level and let it settle back. Water it again, if necessary to resettle the soil.

Drainage

When shallow soil is underlaid by a layer of impervious soil or hardpan, excess water cannot drain away. Here is one solution.

In Layered Soil: Drill through impervious layer with power posthole digger if you can. For thick hardpan, larger power equipment will be needed. Fill the hole with surface soil or soil similar to container mix and plant as usual.

Porous soil →
Hardpan →
Porous soil →

Basins

Build a shallow basin so water soaks down into the rootball with a minimum of run-off. With all of the tree's roots still in the rootball, it will dry faster than surrounding soil.

To improve rooting conditions and save water, build a double basin system. Use the rootball-width basin for primary watering until some roots have grown into the surrounding soil—6 weeks or so. In rainy weather temporarily cut the basin berm so excessive water will drain away.

Row planting

Stretch a string for straight rows. For deep planting furrows, use the corner of a hoe blade. For shallow furrows use the handle. Firm the soil over a seed row with the flat side of a rake.

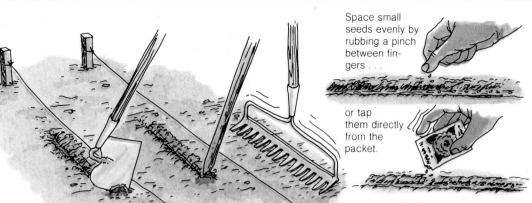

Space small seeds evenly by rubbing a pinch between fingers . . .

or tap them directly from the packet.

Sowing small seeds

When the small size or color of seeds makes them difficult to see as you're sowing, lay sheets of tissue paper in the trench. The tissue will decompose quickly when covered and watered. Seed tape is available for many plants.

A short cut

Save time and expense by using soil mix only in the row or planting hole where you'll put seeds. Make the seed bed at least 3″ wide and 4″ deep.

Planting from cans
(and other containers)

1. Move the tree by holding the can and the trunk near the soil level.

2. Cut the container and lift the tree gently so as not to break the rootball.

Tap tapered containers gently on the sides to loosen soil; then pull the tree out carefully.

3. Cut or pull away any circled or matted roots so they radiate out from the rootball. Shorten roots to the width of the planting hole so they will not be bent when planted.

Cut or straighten roots that circle and remove all matted roots.

Planting balled in burlap

1. Always handle ball carefully. Set in hole with burlap on so the soil line of tree is at the level recommended for your soil.

2. Fill hole gradually with backfill soil, firming it gently with your foot.

3. Cut burlap from around the trunk (or fold it back) and be sure all edges are buried well below the soil surface to prevent wick action from drying out the rootball.

Bareroot planting

1. Before planting trim off any broken or twisted roots or discolored tips. Determine the location of the original soil line—look for soil or a change of color on the trunk.

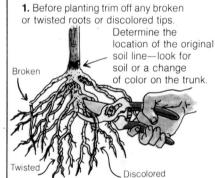

Broken

Twisted

Discolored

2. Set the tree in the hole so the soil line is above the surrounding soil. Spread roots evenly. Keep them radiating out from the root crown— not bent or circled. Work backfill soil between and around the roots.

3. Firm soil gently with a tamp or your foot as you fill the hole, making certain root and soil are in firm contact.

4. Eliminate air pockets, settle soil, and bring soil into firm contact with the roots by running water slowly over root area. Check soil level and build basin as shown on page 82.

Special Handling

The majority of plants grow well when you follow good general gardening practice. But others, described in this chapter, need some special attention if you want the best possible crops or flowers or foliage.

Fruit trees

Fertilizing. Nitrogen is the element most commonly in short supply for fruit trees. Most fruit tree fertilizer will contain higher amounts of nitrogen—for example, 12-6-6 or 12-6-10—than other nutrients.

Since fruit trees are grown in so many different types of soils, it is virtually impossible to pin down the specific fertilizer needs. Also, there are many selections and varieties that respond differently. The trees themselves can often serve as indicators of their needs. If growth is vigorous and healthy and leaves appear normal, then nutrient requirements are being met. But if growth is limited and the leaves are small or pale green or chlorotic, then fertilizer is needed. It's not a good practice to let your trees demonstrate these needs; preventing these deficiencies is a much better practice.

When to feed and how much. For early-bearing trees we suggest applying half the fertilizer in the spring and the other half after harvest. Apply about mid-June for later bearing varieties. Keep the fertilizer at least a foot away from the trunk and apply evenly under the tree canopy.

A general rule of thumb is to use about ¾ pound of nitrogen for each mature tree (not dwarf varieties) per year. This means that for fertilizers having 12% nitrogen, you will need to apply 6 pounds. Young trees will need correspondingly lesser amounts and newly planted trees should not be fertilized with nitrogen until the root system becomes well established. Follow the directions on the fertilizer label.

Potassium and other nutrients. Potassium is commonly deficient in fruit trees—particularly in high rainfall areas and where trees are grown on sandy or gravelly soils. Be sure to include potassium in your fertilizer program under these conditions. Manures contain potash, so this nutrient is added when manures are used.

Phosphorus is very important when the root system is limited. Add phosphorus fertilizer to the planting hole, mixed with the soil.

If after the above, growth is still weak and leaves

Red Bartlett pear

look abnormal, then other nutrients could be deficient—zinc, magnesium, iron, manganese or boron. A foliar spray during the growing season may be the best way of applying these elements.

Feeding with animal manure. Animal manures are suitable tree fertilizers but some care needs to be observed since they often contain harmful amounts of salts and obnoxious weed seeds. Also remember that bird or rabbit manures contain much more nitrogen than cattle or horse manure, so use lesser amounts. About 30 to 60 pounds of bird or rabbit manure or 100 to 200 pounds of cattle manure per tree will supply the nutrient needs

of full-size mature trees. Spread it under the branches in the fall or early spring. For young trees, use ⅓ pound of bird or rabbit manure or one pound of cattle manure per tree one year, doubling this amount each year to maturity.

DWARF AND CONTAINER PLANTINGS
Start out with ¼ cup of a 12-6-6 grade fertilizer (or similar analysis) after the tree is well established. Then repeat this application annually, supplementing it with small additions (⅛ cup increments) every two to three months during the growing season until the tree seems to be doing well. Adjust if growth is too slow or too vigorous.

Water. A standard fruit tree needs deep watering. Dwarf trees on shallow-rooted stocks may not need as much, but any tree must have a constant moisture supply. Here's how to provide it.

At planting time. Water each layer of soil in the planting hole. If the garden soil is dry, soak the hole itself before you put in the plant. Finish by soaking from the top of the planting mound, creating a volcano-like depression to hold the water. Let the hose trickle

Azaleas, one of the most prominent of all flowering shrubs, puts on an incredible show of color in early spring. Azaleas are just one of many plants in the acid-loving group.

so water won't run over the side of the hole.

After planting, and before growth begins, don't water again unless the soil seems unusually dry.

The roots are not in active growth, and soggy soil will cause them to rot.

When growth begins, give a soaking when the top inch or so of soil dries.

Dig down with a trowel and take a look to be sure water is needed. Water with a trickling hose at the top of the planting mound. This is especially important with burlap-wrapped plants, since the soil in the ball may not take up water unless you trickle it straight into the ball.

Shrubs and trees for acid soils:

Amelanchier species:
  Serviceberry (with the exception of several western species)
Arbutus unedo:
  Strawberry tree
Calluna species:
  Heather
Clethra species:
  Summer-sweet, white alder
Cytisus species:
  Broom
Erica species:
  Heath
Gaultheria species:
  Wintergreen, checkerberry, teaberry
Ilex species:
  Holly
Juniperus communis and varieties:
  Common juniper
Kalmia species:
  Laurel
Leiophyllum buxifolium:
  Box sand myrtle
Leucothoe species:
  Leucothoe, fetterbush
Myrica species:
  Myrtle, wax myrtle, candleberry, bayberry
Quercus palustris:
  Pin oak, Spanish oak. Becomes chlorotic on neutral or alkaline soil.
Rhododendron species:
  Rhododendron, azalea
Vaccinium species:
  Blueberry, huckleberry, cranberry, bilberry
Viburnum alnifolium:
  Hobblebush, dogberry, morsewood

Trees for dry soils:

Acacia (most varieties)
Acer negundo:
  Box elder
Ailanthus altissima:
  Tree-of-heaven, varnish tree
Albizia julibrissin:
  Mimosa, silk tree
Arbutus menziesii:
  Madrone
Carpinus caroliniana:
  American hornbeam, blue beech
Carya glabra:
  Pignut hickory, broom hickory
Ceratonia siliqua:
  Carob, St. John's-bread, locust bean
Cercidium floridum:
  Palo verde
Chilopsis linearis:
  Desert willow
Cupressus species:
  Cypress
Elaeagnus angustifolia:
  Russian olive, oleaster
Eucalyptus:
  (most species)
Fraxinus pennsylvanica lanceolata:
  Green ash, red ash
Fraxinus velutina:
  Velvet ash
Juniperus chinensis:
  varieties
Juniperus osteosperma
Juniperus sabina
Juniperus scopulorum
Juniperus virginiana:
  Red cedar
Melia azedarach:
  Chinaberry, Persian lilac
Ostrya virginiana:
  Hop hornbeam
Parkinsonia aculeata:
  Jerusalem thorn
Pinus edulis
Pinus halepensis
Pinus jeffreyi
Pinus ponderosa:
  Ponderosa pine, western yellow pine
Pinus rigida:
  Pitch pine
Pinus sabiniana
Pinus torreyana:
  Torrey pine
Pinus virginiana:
  Virginia pine, scrub pine
Populus alba:
  White poplar, silver-leaved poplar, abele
Populus fremonti:
  Fremont cottonwood
Quercus chrysolepsis
Quercus douglasii
Quercus dumosa
Quercus gambelii
Quercus garryana:
  Oregon oak, western oak
Quercus havardii
Schinus molle:
  California pepper tree
Schinus terebinthifolius:
  Brazilian pepper tree, Christmas-berry tree
Tamarix pentandra
Zizuphys jujuba:
  Common jujube, Chinese date

Trees for wet soils:

Acer rubrum:
  Red maple
Alnus species:
  Alder
Chamaecyparis thyoides:
  White cedar, false cypres
Ilex cassine:
  Dahoon holly
Larix laricina:
  Eastern larch, tamarack
Liquidambar styraciflua:
  American sweet gum, red gum
Magnolia virginiana:
  Sweet bay magnolia
Planera aquatica:
  Water elm
Populus:
  Poplars, aspen, cottonwood. Most species will grow on wet soils.
Quercus alba
Quercus palustris:
  Pin oak, Spanish oak
Quercus phellos
Salix species:
  Willow
Taxodium distichum:
  Bald cypress
Umbellularia californica:
  Cajeput tree, California bay, California laurel

Trees for gravelly soils:

Abies nordmanniana:
  Nordmann fir. Will grow on gravelly hardpan.
Ailanthus altissima:
  Tree-of-heaven, varnish tree
Albizia julibrissin:
  Mimosa, silk tree
Broussonetia papyrifera:
  Paper mulberry, tapa-cloth tree
Gleditsia triacanthos:
  Honey locust, sweet locust
Pinus mugo:
  Mugho pine, mountain pine
Quercus garryana:
  Oregon oak, western oak
Sassafras albidum:
  Sassafras

Trees for dry, alkaline soils in the West:

Acer negundo
Albizia julibrissin:
  Silk tree, mimosa
Celtis reticulata
Cercocarpus ledifolius
Elaeagnus augustifolia
Fraxinus velutina:
  Velvet ash
Koelreuteria paniculata:
  Golden-rain tree
Populus fremonti:
  Fremont cottonwood
Robinia pseudoacacia
Sophora japonica:
  Japanese pagoda
Zizyphus jujuba:
  Common jujube, Chinese date

Trees for alkaline soils in the East:

Fagus:
  Beech
Franklinia alatamaha:
  Franklin tree. Prefers slightly alkaline and moist but well-drained soil.
Juniperus virginiana:
  Red cedar

Trees and shrubs for very sandy soils:

Ailanthus altissima:
  Tree-of-heaven, varnish tree
Albizia julibrissin:
  Mimosa, silk tree
Cupressus arizonica bonita:
  Smooth Arizona cypress
Grevillea robusta:
  Silk oak
Juniperus chinensis pfitzerana:
  Pfitzer juniper
Juniperus conferta:
  Shore juniper
Juniperus horizontalis:
  Creeping juniper, creeping cedar
Juniperus sabina:
  Savin juniper
Leptospermum laevigatum:
  Australian tea tree
Parkinsonia aculeata:
  Jerusalem thorn
Pinus rigida:
  Pitch pine
Pinus sylvestris:
  Scotch pine

When first-season growth is abundant. In midsummer, when the tree is growing well, stop watering from the top of the mound. Create a shallow ditch right at the base of the planting mound and soak the soil in this circular ditch about every two to three weeks, or when the top inch or two dries.

Watering after the first season. Make a shallow ditch about 6 to 12 inches wide in a circle that's just outside the tips of the branches. Move the ditch outward as the tree grows. Soak thoroughly about once every 3 to 4 weeks. This is an approximate guide: your tree may need water every 2 weeks in very sandy soil, or not for 6 weeks in heavy soil. Make it a practice to dig down to check the moisture in the upper few inches before watering. Conserve the water by spreading a 2-inch layer of mulch over the roots from the mound area to the outside of the watering ditch.

How long to water. You want to soak the soil long enough to force water down to the deep roots of a fruit tree. On dwarf trees the deepest roots may stop 30 to 36 inches below the surface. On big trees, the roots may extend many feet. Remember, too, that water sinks quickly through sandy soil but very slowly through clay. A day after you've kept the watering ditch full for 2 or 3 hours, check penetration by pushing a 4 or 5-foot length of stiff wire into the soil. When it refuses to go down any farther, pull it out and check the depth of penetration. Soil should be moist down to at least 2½ feet for dwarfs, 3½ to 4 feet for big trees. Do not place mulch next to the tree trunk, thus avoiding danger of collar rots and rodent damage.

Trees in a lawn area should have a deep soak about twice a summer, in addition to the lawn watering.

Tangelo

CITRUS

The rewards for the citrus grower are many: attractive glossy foliage, delicious and beautiful fruit, and fragrant flowers. Where they are climatically adapted, citrus are among the most satisfying plants in the garden. But they require a little extra care.

Citrus are sensitive to too much or too little water. Provide a constant supply of moisture but make sure the drainage is excellent. Citrus will not tolerate poor drainage. A layer of organic mulch will help keep the moisture supply even. If your natural soil is heavy and retains most of the water applied to it, plant citrus in raised beds, on mounds, or in containers.

Don't let water stand around the trunk of citrus plants. If you build a basin, keep 6 inches of dry soil around the trunk, and make the outer basin extend past the drip line. It's not advisable to use a citrus as a lawn tree, but if one is growing in your lawn, leave at least a 2-foot buffer zone of open soil between the grass and trunk.

If you plant citrus in containers, remember to compensate for the restricted root space with additional water and regular applications of fertilizer.

Fertilization is important with citrus, and most varieties respond to a formula that is high in nitro-

gen and also contains the various trace elements or micronutrients. Citrus in containers need feedings once a month because regular waterings tend to leach the nutrients out of the pot. Citrus in the open ground need three feedings a year—in late winter, and mid and late summer.

Citrus often suffer from iron chlorosis (see page 52) or zinc deficiency which shows up as yellow veins in otherwise dark green leaves. There are several commercial formulations that will quickly correct chlorosis and zinc deficiencies. Check at your garden center and follow label directions.

Small Fruits

GRAPES

Grapes send their roots very deep—as deep as the soil permits. To encourage deep rooting, water slowly to a depth of 3 feet during the growing season. With heavy or shallow soils, you should make the best of them by digging in plenty of organic matter at planting time and mulching the soil afterward.

Use a complete fertilizer on grape vines, and let the color and growth rate determine the frequency and amount of applica-

Gewürztraminer grapes

tion. Vines should have green leaves, not yellow, and should grow well through early summer. Too much fertilizer late in the season will encourage lush growth during the ripening period and may damage the crop on the vine and the buds for the following season.

STRAWBERRIES

If you're going to grow strawberries in garden soil or in containers, ask for plants that are certified as disease-free.

Plant strawberries in soil with good drainage. Mound the planting site if you're not sure about the drainage. At the proper planting depth, the new leaf bud in the center of each plant should sit exactly level with the soil surface.

Gardeners who grow strawberries in containers in a disease-free soil mix don't have to worry about verticillium wilt and red stele (root rot). Both are caused by soil-borne fungus.

Winter protection is needed where alternate freezing and thawing of the soil may cause the plants to heave and break the roots. Low temperatures also injure the crowns of the plants. Straw is one of the best mulch materials.

Place straw 3 or 4 inches deep over the plants before the soil is frozen hard. Remove most of the mulch in spring when the center of a few plants shows a yellow-green color. You can leave an inch of loose straw or even add some fresh straw between rows. The plants will come up through it and it will help retain moisture in the soil and keep mud off the berries.

Vegetables

ASPARAGUS

Soil. When planting asparagus seed you are building the foundation for 10 to 15 years of production —so take the time to work the soil to a depth of a foot or more and mix in large amounts of manure, compost, peat moss or similar organic material, plus 4 to 5 pounds of 5-10-10 fertilizer per 100 square feet.

When you plant transplants (root crowns), you save a year over starting from seed by buying one-year-old plants (crowns). They're usually available in late winter or early spring from garden centers or seed companies.

Dig trenches 8 inches deep and 4 to 5 feet apart (asparagus roots reach wide). Spread some compost or manure in the bottom of the trench and cover with an inch of garden soil.

New asparagus spears

Set the crowns 18 inches apart in the row and cover with 2 inches of soil. As the new shoots come up, gradually fill in the trench.

Fertilizer and water. For high production and thick spears, follow a twice-a-year feeding program. Make one application before growth starts in the spring and the second as soon as the harvest is finished to encourage heavy top growth.

Don't skimp on water when the top growth is developing

Harvest. Cut or snap off spears when 6 to 8 inches high. "Snapping" —bending the spear over sharply until it breaks —avoids injury to other shoots below ground. When cutting spears, the asparagus knife is a handy tool.

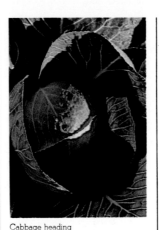

Cabbage heading

CABBAGE

Cabbage is a heavy user of nitrogen and potash. Before planting add 6 to 8 pounds of 5-10-10 per 100 square feet and work it into the soil. Follow up, in 3 to 4 weeks, with a side dressing of about 1 pound of ammonium nitrate per 100 feet of row.

To slow up splitting, hold off on water or partially root-prune the plant when the heads are formed. Some gardeners simply twist the plant to break some of the roots. Splitting is seldom a problem with later varieties maturing in cool weather.

CARROTS

In the Nichols Nursery Catalog, from Albany, Oregon, you'll find this paragraph headlined "How to raise carrots without using a spade or hoe. It is simple, and here is how it is done:

"Build a raised bed made of 2 by 8 lumber (length optional) but width

Carrots fresh from the garden

should not exceed 4 feet. Fill bed with 1/5 garden loam, 2/5 clean sand and 2/5 compost, rotted manure, or peat moss. For every 100 foot length of bed, spread 5 pounds of bone meal. Mix thoroughly all ingredients, then rake down into a fine seedbed. Broadcast the carrot seed, cover with ¼-inch fine sifted peat moss. Water, and keep bed well moistened, but not soggy wet. Pull carrots as they are ready. July sown seed will give you carrots in the fall."

The only question we have about the above soil mix is the possibility of using manure. Manures, unless very well rotted, cause roughness and branching in carrots, and may be a source of wireworms.

The raised bed reduces cracking and decay caused by excess water in the fall. Digging is no trouble in the light soil mix. Soil warms up early in raised beds and carrots can be started sooner than the regular garden soil can be worked.

Celery ready to harvest

CELERY AND CELERIAC

Celery demands more time and attention than most vegetables. If you don't start with transplants from the garden store, you have a 10 to 12 week growing period indoors or about 4 months in the garden.

Heavy applications of fertilizer are necessary: as much as 16 pounds of 5-10-10 per 100 feet of row.

These quantities must be thoroughly mixed into a wide row to avoid burning.

Celery must have an abundant and continuous water supply.

Celeriac grows in the same way as celery. It demands as much fertilizer and a continuous supply of water.

BELGIAN ENDIVE

Seeds are sown in early summer and require 5 months to produce the roots, which are grown like parsnips. Do not plant too early. A plant that goes to seed is useless for the next step, called forcing. The roots are dug in the fall and the tops cut off 2 inches above the root crown to prevent injury to crown buds. The roots are stored in a cool place and subsequently forced at room temperatures of 60°F to 70°F (16°C to 21°C) as follows:

The tips of the roots are cut so they are uniform in length, about 6 to 9 inches. They are set in an upright position in a trench or box with the crown up. The space between the roots is filled with soil. After thoroughly wetting the soil the entire vegetable—root and crown—is covered with sand to a depth of 6 to 8 inches. The soil should be kept moist. The sand keeps the heads compact and excludes light, to cause blanching. About 3 to 4 weeks are required to produce good heads weighing 2 to 3 ounces and measuring 4 to 6 inches tall. Medium-size roots (1 to 1¾ inches in diameter) produce the largest yield. Small roots produce low yields and large roots produce compound heads.

CORN

Fertilizer. The following is a fertilization schedule that works very well for corn:

At planting time, fertilize in bands on both sides of seed row, 2 inches from seed in the furrow

Corn tassels

and an inch deeper than seed level. Use 3 pounds of 5-10-10 (in each band) per 100 feet of row.

When corn is 8 inches high, side-dress with same amount. Repeat when knee high (18 inches).

Nitrogen deficiency is easy to spot because the lower leaves of the plants turn yellow very quickly.

Water. It's water all the way for corn. Here are a few points to remember:

The water need is greatest from tasseling time to picking time.

Sweet corn makes very rapid growth during the time the ears are maturing. No check in watering should occur during this period.

In very hot and dry weather, rolling of the leaves may occur in midday even when soil moisture is adequate. Plants will transpire water faster than the roots will absorb water. But if leaves roll (edges turn upward), check the soil for moisture.

CUCUMBER

Cucumbers respond to generous amounts of organic matter in the soil. For special treatment, dig the planting furrow 2 feet deep and fill the first foot or so with manure mixed with peat moss, compost, sawdust or other organic material. Fill up the furrow with soil, peat moss and 5-10-10 fertilizer at the rate of 2 pounds to 50 feet of row.

Since cucumber roots will grow to a depth of 3 feet if the soil is normal, watering should be slow and deep. If the plant is under stress from lack of moisture at any time, it just stops growing. It will pick up again when moisture is supplied. It is normal for leaves of cucumbers to temporarily wilt in the middle of the day during hot spells, but check below the surface of the soil for moisture.

LETTUCE

Lettuce occupies the soil for a relatively short time, and every day must be a growing day with an adequate supply of nutrients and moisture.

Fertilize soil before planting with 3 or 4 pounds of 5-10-10 per 100 square feet. If the growth of a young plant is checked by lack of nutrients, it never fully recovers.

Lettuce ready for picking

Never let the plant suffer from lack of moisture. The period of greatest need is when the heads begin to develop.

ONIONS

Onions are heavy feeders. Work manure and synthetic fertilizer into the soil before planting. A pound of manure to each square foot of ground and 4 to 5 pounds of 5-10-10 fertilizer per 100 square feet will do the job.

A constant supply of moisture is essential. It is especially important during the bulb enlargement stage. New growth stops

from the center when bulbing starts.

PARSNIPS

Roots develop to a length of 12 to 18 inches and become distorted in a heavy rough soil. The parsnip therefore is best when grouped with carrots and salsify in a raised bed or in deeply dug soil to which generous amounts of organic matter have been added.

Roots will take from 100 to 120 days to mature and must be subjected to winter cold—near the freezing point—to change the starch to sugar and give it the sweet nutlike flavor it's famous for.

Parsnip roots may be left in the ground all winter or dug out in the late fall and stored in moist sand. They can stand alternate freezing and thawing in the soil but are definitely damaged if frozen after harvest.

POTATO

The usual planting method is to set seed pieces, cut side down, 4 inches deep and 12 inches apart in rows 24 to 36 inches apart. The tubers (what you eat) form on many stems rising from the seed piece. The potatoes do not grow in the roots. They form above the seed piece on underground stems

Apply fertilizer in bands at both sides of the seed pieces at planting time. The best method is to make a trench 3 inches deep and 6 inches wide. Place seed pieces in a row down the center and work in fertilizer 1 to 2 inches deep at the edges of the trench.

When the plants are 5 to 6 inches high, scrape soil from between the rows and hill up the plants, covering the stems with soil. Tubers exposed to light, either in the garden or storage, turn green and become inedible.

Potatoes need a steady supply of moisture. If the soil dries out after the

tubers begin to form, a second growth starts when the soil becomes moist. The result is knobby potatoes or multiples. Alternate wet and dry conditions will cause "hollow heart" or cavities near the center of the tuber.

Other mistakes are over-fertilizing before the tubers are formed, ignoring the best planting dates and permitting the tubers to turn green from exposure.

Uncovering new potatoes

An old-time method of growing potatoes that you pick rather than dig is this: Set seed pieces in a wide trench 3 inches deep, and as the stems grow, build up a covering of straw, pine needles or any material that will protect them from the sun. (Cover the material with half an inch of soil if wind is a problem.) The potatoes will form almost at ground level and can be picked up by pulling back the straw. Early potatoes can be picked when tops begin to flower. They will reach full size when the tops die down. One potato vine will yield from 6 to 8 pounds of potatoes.

SALSIFY

Salsify, like carrots and parsnips, is at its best in a raised bed filled with a special mix of organic matter, fine sand and vermiculite or perlite.

SWEET POTATO

Sweet potatoes need a light sandy soil. When grown in heavy soils, the

Sweet potatoes

enlarged roots are apt to be long and stringy.

Too much water tends to make the roots more elongated and less blocky.

Fertilization is tricky. With too much nitrogen, sweet potatoes develop more vines than roots. However, it's not a crop that does well in poor soil. Additions of a low nitrogen fertilizer, such as 5-10-10, worked into the soil at the rate of 4 pounds to 100 feet of row will improve the yield. Prepare the soil 2 weeks before planting.

TOMATOES

Soil. The general rule in transplanting is "never plant deeper than it grew in the nursery." The exception to this rule is the tomato plant which has the ability to develop roots along the stem wherever the stem comes in contact with moist soil. For that reason, set any tomato transplant deep in the soil—up to its first leaves.

Fertilizer. The first step in any fertilization program for tomatoes is to give the roots of the newly set-out plants ready access to a generous supply of phosphorus. This element does not drain through the soil as nitrogen and potassium do. Therefore, it must be placed where the newly formed roots can get to it.

First fertilizing. There are three ways to satisfy the high phosphorus requirement of the newly set-out plant in garden soil:
(1) Mix a timed-release, high-phosphorus fertilizer thoroughly into the soil in the area to be planted. Apply the dry fertilizer at the specified rate per foot of row (or 1 pound for 10 feet of row with the 5-10-10 formula) and spread the fertilizer over the area to be planted; mix into the top 6 inches of the soil. This one application of a timed-release fertilizer will take care of the plant throughout the growing season. It also works for containerized plants in ordinary soil.
(2) Side-dress transplants with a high-phosphorus fertilizer just before or at the time of planting. Apply in narrow bands or furrows 3 to 4 inches away from the center of the transplant hole in a trench 3 inches deep.
(3) Apply a starter solution when setting out transplants. Prepare holes large enough and deep enough to receive the plants. In a pail, dilute a high-phosphorus fertilizer according to label directions. Pour the solution in each planting hole at the recommended rate.

Vine-ripe tomatoes

Follow-up. The tomato plant has a lot of work to do. Clusters of fruit call for an abundant food supply. Nutrients and moisture must be constantly available for continuous leaf growth and fruit development. So, once the fruit has set, you should apply fertilizer once or twice a month if you haven't used a timed-release fertilizer at planting time.

All vine and no fruit. The tomato plant may fail to change gears from the vegetative stage to the fruiting stage. Too much nitrogen fertilizer and too much water in the first stage of growth is one cause of the failure. Too much shade is another. You can help the plant switch over to the fruiting stage by plucking out the terminal shoots, or by withholding water to check growth, or even by root pruning. And by following a fertilizing schedule suggested here.

Choose one of these ways to fertilize:

Program 1 — *Planting in garden soil.*
1. Use a fertilizer high in phosphorous before planting.
2. Use a starter solution —also high in phosphorous—when setting out transplants.
3. When fruit is set, use the same fertilizer as in Step 1.
4. Follow up with applications, once or twice a month, of the same fertilizer as Steps 1 and 3.

Program 2 — *Planting in garden soil.*
1. Same as Program 1.
2. Same as Program 1.
3. When fruit is set, apply a complete fertilizer.
4. Follow-up application once or twice a month with same fertilizer as Step 3.

Program 3 — *Planting in containers with synthetic soil.*
1. Nutrients in soil mix take care of the first 2 to 3 weeks.
2. Start regular feeding program making applications according to size of container and frequency of watering. For example, a 5-gallon container would be fertilized more frequently than a 10-gallon container.

Program 4 — *Planting in garden or container with timed-release fertilizer.*
1. Mix timed-release fertilizer with soil when setting out transplants. Follow manufacturer's label instructions.
2. This single application takes care of the plant throughout the growing season.

WATERCRESS

Watercress can be grown from either seed or cuttings. You can take cuttings from the watercress you buy at the market. Stick them in sand or planter mix in a pot. Set in a tub of water.

Watercress seed is very small. Sow in small containers and transplant when 2 or 3 inches tall. If you can supply enough water to keep the soil continuously moist—perhaps by a drip method—you can grow watercress in a cold frame, planter box or in a trench.

If you have a small stream or spring suitable for watercress, you'll find detailed information on growing in *"Commercial Growing of Watercress"* (Farmers Bulletin No. 2233), Superintendent of Documents, Washington, D.C. 20402.

Ornamentals

THE ACID-LOVERS

We've grouped many plants with similar requirements under the common heading of the "acid-lovers." They're rather particular about water, soil and fertilizer, and distinctive in their need for an acid soil.

Plants in this group include rhododendrons (including azaleas), camellias, *Pieris, Ternstroemia,* daphne, gardenias, *Nandina* and certain ferns. Most gardeners agree that the acid-lovers are a special group of plants worthy of special attention.

The number-one requirement is a soil rich with organic soil amendments—preferably slightly acid amendments such as peat moss. This requirement is important because most of the acid-lovers need plenty of moisture, but also need a very high proportion of air in the soil. Organic matter helps create a soil that retains moisture and at the same time allows sufficient air in the soil after watering. Many commercial growers grow rhododendrons and azaleas in pure, coarse peat moss. If you're serious about success with these plants, don't skimp on the organic matter.

Rhododendron intricatum

Most of the acid-lovers concentrate their roots near the surface of the soil, which, of course, is the first layer of soil to dry out. This rooting characteristic influences much of the care given these plants by sensitive gardeners: (1) Never cultivate around these plants; you'll destroy much of the root system. (2) Watch your watering closely so the plants never have a chance to fully dry out; if you water by flooding instead of overhead sprinkling, you'll reduce the transference of disease from flower to soil and vice versa. And (3) Keep a 1 or 2-inch mulch of organic matter around the root zone at all times: it can save a plant from a lapse in regular watering and protect the surface roots from excess heat. With camellias, keep the mulch 2 inches from the trunk of the plant to avoid rot and disease.

And lastly, feed these special plants with fertilizers specially formulated for them. There are both liquid and dry forms of fertilizers that are acid in reaction; one form is not necessarily better than

another, so use the one which suits your gardening habits. Feeding should be done, according to the manufacturer's directions, on a monthly schedule throughout the growing season (from early spring to August in most areas).

Some specialists say that feeding with a 0-10-10 formula during the dormant season produces bigger and better flowers the following season.

BEGONIAS

Both the large flowered tuberous begonias and the smaller flowered fibrous begonias used for bedding need a soil made rich with the addition of lots of leaf mold, coarse peat or ground bark. In fact, many growers who specialize in tuberous begonias use a mixture of leaf mold, peat and bark, or use one of the ingredients, straight, as a potting mix. Because begonias need ample moisture—soil that is constantly damp but not wet—whatever mix you use must have exceptional drainage or the tubers or

Fibrous begonia bed

plants will rot. A regular feeding program will reward the grower with an abundance of flowers. The best bet is to feed monthly with a complete fertilizer.

CAMELLIAS

Camellias are members of the acid-loving group. They require: rich soil with plenty of organic matter, good drainage,

and regular feedings with an acid fertilizer.

In addition to meeting these general requirements, take precautions

Camellia blossoms

not to plant camellias too deep—keep the base of the trunk above the soil line. The addition of an organic mulch helps camellias in many ways, but don't get it too close to the trunk.

DAPHNE

Daphne has a reputation for being a finicky grower and, unfortunately, the reputation is well deserved. The best advice is to plant in a soil that cannot be overwatered—a light soil with plenty of organic matter. During the summer, let daphnes dry out a little between waterings. Supplied with the proper soil and careful watering, daphne may surprise the gardener with its vigor.

FUCHSIA

For the best performance, give fuchsias the personalized attention they require in the soil, fertilizer and water categories.

Soil. The best bet is to use a commercial mix, one based on either the University of California or the Cornell formula (see page 40). These mixes satisfy fuchsia's need for a rich soil that is fast-draining but water-retentive.

Fertilizer. Liquid fertilizers, especially fish emulsion, work best with fuchsias. Apply at slightly

Fuchsia 'Little Surprise'

weaker than the recommended dilutions, and apply more often— every 10 to 14 days.

Water. A soil mix that drains well is absolutely essential because it's almost impossible to overwater fuchsias during their growing season— especially if grown in containers. If grown in the soil, a thick organic mulch will help fuchsia retain the moisture they need.

GARDENIAS

Gardenias, like daphne, rank among the most finicky ornamental shrubs. But the rewards, in flowers and scents, more than make up for the extra care they require.

Plant gardenias in a light soil that drains well, adding plenty of peat moss or ground bark to the surrounding soil. Plant slightly higher than you would other ornamentals to avoid puddling around the base of the plant, and add a good layer of organic mulch to the surface. Soil should be kept on the moist side. Feed with a fertilizer for acid-lovers every 3 to 4 weeks during the flowering season.

GERANIUMS
(Pelargonium)

Common geraniums can sometimes give gardeners a problem. They'll do well in most garden soils but prefer a light soil that drains well. If you're planting geraniums in

Old-fashioned geraniums

pots, mix in a little extra peat moss or ground bark —they prefer a soil that is neutral to slightly acid. Don't overwater geraniums, even those in pots; and for best bloom allow plants to become somewhat potbound. Geraniums are not heavy feeders; too much nitrogen may cause more leaves than flowers.

HYDRANGEAS

In area with mild winters, hydrangeas—especially the old-fashioned garden hydrangea *(H. macrophylla)*—are among the most spectacular flowering plants to be found. Gardeners either love their oversized clusters of pink to red to blue flowers, or can't stand them.

Hydrangea macrophylla

If you're a hydrangea admirer, plant them in a cool spot in a rich porous soil and give them plenty of water. Pink and red flowering varieties *(H. macrophylla)* can be made to turn a rich blue color by making the soil acid with the addition of aluminum sulfate (available at garden supply stores).

If you want pink or red flowers, keep the soil neutral or on the alkaline side (for more information on changing soil pH, see page 26). Applications of any substance to influence the color of the flowers should be started in spring before the flowers appear.

LILIES

Lilies are among the most beautiful of all the flowering bulbs, and the addition of many recent hybrids has made the selection even more spectacular. As is the case with most spectacular plants, lilies require some extra care.

White lilies

The old-timer's advice on growing lilies was to plant them "with their feet in the shade and their heads in the sun." This is still sound advice, but it isn't always easy to provide lilies with those exact conditions. To grow good lilies, you must have a deep, rich and well-drained soil. If your soil is not so good, spend a little extra time preparing a bed just for lilies, using plenty of organic matter, or plant them in a raised bed. The soil should be

loose and friable to a depth of at least 12 inches. Keep the soil constantly moist, but never wet, and keep the roots cool with the addition of a thick organic mulch. Feed lilies with a complete, mild fertilizer on a monthly schedule during the growing season.

ROSES

The rose is a high-powered manufacturing plant. To allow it to develop its full power, it must have a continuous supply of water in the root zone and plenty of the nutrients for good foliage and flower production.

Your plant must have a profusion of leaves if it's expected to bear lots of beautiful roses. It takes 25 to 35 perfect leaves to create one perfect rosebud and bring it into bloom.

Roses in the garden

Water. One thing rose growers do agree on is that you can't give a rose too much water. But a rose will not tolerate wet feet: drainage must be excellent.

Rose foliage will wilt if water is insufficient. Always keep the plant moist enough that the leaves will be distended with water, or "moisture-turgid."

We can't tell you how much or how often to water—the frequency of watering, as well as the amount, depends on soil characteristics, climate, and the growth stage of the rose. More water is needed when the soil is loose and sandy, when it's heavily compacted, when the air is hot and dry, or when new plants are developing.

Normally a rose should receive the equivalent of 1 inch of rainfall per week, all at one time, starting in early spring and continuing through fall. Hot and dry weather may call for watering every 3 or 4 days, or oftener during drought.

Even when rainfall is plentiful, porous soils benefit from additional deep soakings.

In the early spring, water the plant from overhead early in the day to prevent canes from drying while developing. When foliage growth begins, keep water off the leaves and apply directly to the soil for best results.

When you water, water well, soaking the soil to a depth of 8 to 10 inches. A light sprinkling is worse than no water at all. Frequent light applications result in shallow root systems and increased susceptibility to injury from drought.

Professional rose growers cannot agree on the correct method of watering. You have a choice —sprinkling or several forms of irrigation.

Some people build a basin or dike around the entire rose bed; others prefer a basin around each bush. Either way, the basin is flooded with water that slowly soaks into the soil. This is a good method in regions with very dry summers.

The most efficient system seems to be slow-drip irrigation at the base of the plants. A heavy stream of water from a hose is wasteful, because most of it runs off and what remains penetrates the soil only a few inches. Also, water and mud splashed on the leaves spread disease-causing organisms. A soaker hose, or one of the methods illustrated on page 79, can soak the soil to the required depth. Also, a soaker hose does not wet the foliage or spread the mulch, thus reducing disease. It saves you time, energy and even money, because less water is used in the long run.

If you do choose to sprinkle, however, water early in the morning so the leaves can dry before they are exposed to the hot midday sun. Be sure the sprinkler runs long enough to meet the requirement for an 8 to 10-

inch deep soak. With this method you'll have to make more frequent application of fungicides to guard against mildew and blackspot.

Fertilizer. A rose is a heavy user of nutrients. Regular applications of fertilizer are required for optimum growth.

The rate, frequency and kind of fertilizer depend on the type of soil. Plants in sandy soils benefit from frequent applications; those in heavy soils may not need as much.

Begin your fertilizer program for newly planted bushes after the plants become established— about 3 or 4 weeks after planting.

Climbing rose

Some rose people advocate 3 applications per year for hybrid teas, grandifloras and floribundas:
(1) In early spring just after pruning, when the bush begins to leaf out.
(2) In early summer, when the plant is beginning to flower.
(3) In late summer, to carry the plant on through fall. In warm coastal areas, an additional application in the fall may be necessary.

One application a year, early in the spring before the leaves come out, may be enough for climbers and shrub species. But the majority of rosarians agree on more frequent applications for all types of roses. Begin in early spring as the bush puts out leaves, then continue to feed every six weeks or even once each month through late summer.

Liquid food is the favor-

ite of many rose growers. Others prefer liquid only for newly planted bushes, applied every 2 to 3 weeks until the plant is established. Then they switch to granular fertilizers for a regular diet.

When using liquid rose food, follow the label directions for mixing. Unless the product is recommended for foliar feeding, wash off any liquid fertilizer that gets on the foliage.

Some rose growers combine foliar feeding with regular pesticide spraying every 2 weeks. The addition of some foliar food just before the peak of the blooming season can result in roses of exhibition quality.

Do not apply foliar food in hot weather. (See Foliar Feeding, page 71.)

If you select granular fertilizers, be sure to wet the soil before applying. Apply about 6 inches away from the main stem. Distribute the prescribed amount uniformly out beyond branch spread and work into the surface of soil or mulch. Water well after application.

Over-fertilizing can leave deposits of salts in the soil that cause stunted growth, off-color foliage, and death of new foliage. If you feel you have over-fertilized, water heavily to put the fertilizer salts in suspension, then follow by another heavy watering to leach them away from the bush.

Roses in containers

Water. Keep the soil in containers evenly moist at all times during the growing season. Usually twice-a-week watering is sufficient but the plant may require daily watering during a hot spell. The more active its growth, the more water it will require.

Fertilize the plant weekly with liquid plant food. Use at half strength until good growth is established, then increase to full strength as recommended on the label. If you prefer, you can apply

timed-release fertilizers every 6 weeks, either alone or in combination with systemic pesticides.

Succulents

Soil. For growing succulents in containers, a good start is a packaged sterilized potting soil. You can find several brands —all of which are good —at garden centers and nurseries. They have the advantage of coming in convenient sizes and being disease-, pest-, and weed-free.

Consider a packaged soil your basic ingredient, but not a complete mix for succulents—it retains too much moisture for succulents when used by itself. You can substitute good garden loam if you have it available, or your local nursery may offer its own sterilized garden soil, which will do as well.

Good drainage is a must and coarse sand will provide aeration and drainage. Be sure to get a coarse grade; fine sand packs down hard, eliminating air spaces. It also crusts over on the surface, making it hard for water to penetrate. Don't use beach sand; it's much too fine and (from the seashore) too salty.

Many growers use sponge rock because it is lightweight and does not compact. The soil remains porous and fast-draining. Succulents are, as a rule, slow-growing plants and do not need to be repotted frequently unless the soil compacts and drainage becomes poor.

Sponge rock does have one inconvenient feature; it is so lightweight that it floats off the surface of the soil when you water. A fine grade of crushed volcanic rock is slightly heavier. Like sponge rock, it does not break down in the soil and will provide fast drainage over a period of years. It is available at garden centers in either black or red; except for the color, there is no difference between the two.

Other substitutes for coarse sand are perlite, silt-free decomposed granite, and coarsely crushed charcoal. Pet stores carry activated charcoal in small amounts and farm supply stores stock poultry charcoal. Agricultural pumice (mined from an area in the California desert) is preferred by many commercial succulent growers instead of coarse sand or perlite. It does not break down, so it permanently prohibits soil shrinkage or compacting. It is stable in the pot and won't float like perlite or wash down like sand.

The last good ingredient in soil for succulents is leaf mold or a similar compost. This gives the potting mix bulk and texture, and releases small amounts of nutrients to the plant over a considerable period of time. If leaf mold isn't available, you can substitute coarse sphagnum moss; you'll find it at nurseries and garden centers. Note: sphagnum moss and peat moss are not the same, and peat moss will *not* do: it's too acidic and it compacts, retaining moisture too long.

Using these ingredients, you can make up a potting soil that will suit any succulent by varying the proportions of each ingredient. The three soil mixes recommended here will take care of the needs of a wide variety of species.

Basic formulas
#1 Extra-lean:
　(A very low-nutrient
　　formula)
　2 parts coarse sand or
　　Agricultural pumice
　1 part potting soil
#2 Regular:
　(A general formula)
　1 part coarse sand or
　　Agricultural pumice
　1 part potting soil
　1 part leaf mold
#3 Extra-rich:
　(A high-nutrient formula)
　1 part coarse sand or
　　Agricultural pumice
　1 part potting soil
　2 parts leaf mold

Cactus and succulent collection

Fertilizer. Because succulents grow slowly, most of them don't need additional fertilizer. The exceptions are the tree-dwelling jungle succulents— the spathiphyllum, rhipsalis, or schlumbergera (zygo-cactus). These thrive on a diet of liquid fertilizer applied at half the recommended strength as a foliar spray (see page 71) very early in the day. This can be repeated every 2 weeks during the active growing period. Never apply fertilizer when a plant is dormant, and don't foliar feed when in bloom.

When a succulent is ready for repotting— when the roots have filled the pot and the soil is depleted—it's a good time for very light feeding. Actually, new soil contains sufficient nutrients for most succulent plants. But since some experts we know also feed their plants at repotting time, we'll pass on their methods. Some simply water the plant thoroughly a week or so after repotting and then apply a liquid fertilizer at half strength. One experienced grower adds bone meal to the soil mix at the rate of one teaspoonful to each 6-inch pot. Because it breaks down over a very long time and re-

leases its nutrients to the plant very slowly, bone meal is considered by this grower as the only safe fertilizer for cacti. Stronger feeding can promote weak, soft growth that is vulnerable to pests and diseases; slow, sturdy growth is healthier, and produces show-quality specimens.

In landscape plants, you can use about 4 pounds of bone meal for every 100 square feet of soil, digging it into the soil at the time of planting.

Another successful grower soaks 1 pound of cottonseed meal in 5 gallons of water for a period of 24 hours, then skims off the clear liquid at the top and pours it at the base of container plants that are not to be repotted at that time. This is a regular spring ritual, along with any necessary repotting chores. This grower also uses the liquid as a foliary spray for his schlumbergeras (zygo-cacti).

Whatever the experts use to feed their plants, they all observe these five rules religiously:
1. Never fertilize a plant during dormancy.
2. Never fertilize a sick plant.
3. Never fertilize a plant that is not rooted.
4. Never fertilize a plant

that has just been repotted. (Incorporating bone meal into the soil mix is the one exception.)
5. Always water a plant before fertilizing, even when applying a liquid fertilizer.

Landscape plantings to which new soil is added can be fed with a commercial liquid fertilizer diluted to half the strength recommended on the label. If leaf mold is available, mix in a little bone meal with the leaf mold (1 to 30 ratio) and use it as a mulch.

Water. How the water is applied to succulents is important. The best way to water landscape plantings is by slow irrigation. The best way to water succulents in pots is to plunge them to the rim in a bucket of water and immerse them until they stop bubbling. The bubbles are from the air that is pushed to the surface of the soil as the water fills the air pockets in the soil. When the soil is saturated, set the pot on a wire rack or a bed of crushed rock or gravel to drain thoroughly. Don't set the pot in a saucer—the water may collect and succulents don't like to sit in puddles.

As a general rule, overhead sprinkling is

not a good way to water succulents. Excess moisture might remain on the plant, exposing it to rot and other forms of fungus. Regular overhead watering can remove the "bloom" (powder) that is an attractive feature of many succulents as well as a natural protection against excessive light absorption. The salts present in some water sources can also cause spotting on foliage and, unfortunately, the damage may be permanent. The powder is not replaced if it is disturbed.

There are occasions when overhead sprinkling is beneficial. Done on warm summer mornings, it's a good way to rinse off dust and dirt, and discourage summer pests. But be careful when spraying those plants that have a powdery coating that you don't spray too hard. Watering on warm mornings will permit the soil to dry out a little before temperatures drop in the evening.

Most city water naturally contains a portion of salt. These salts can concentrate in the soil, especially in potted plants, and sometimes appear on the sides and rims of clay pots as crusty white deposits. These concentrated salts can burn plant tissues, especially the delicate feeder roots.

There are several ways to prevent this. You can use rainwater, well water or spring water, if available. Or, you can make a practice of leaching out your pots every third time you water. Leaching consists simply of pouring water through the soil from top to bottom at least three times and allowing it to drain each time. This rinses the salts out of the soil and out of the pores of the porous pots.

The visible effects of salt burn on plants are brown tips on the leaves. Salt burns can also damage roots and can weaken the whole plant. One important warning: don't use chemically softened water on any plant. Softened water has a high sodium content and will damage your plants severely.

In general, water your succulents thoroughly, then let them dry out. Water early in the day so that most of the surface water will have evaporated by the time evening temperatures begin to drop. If you overhead-sprinkle, keep plants out of direct sun until the surface droplets evaporate. Remember that moisture and cool temperatures are an open invitation to various forms of rot in succulents.

Other Shrubs and Trees

BAMBOO

Although most gardeners try to limit the growth and spread of the various bamboos, there are those who don't. Here's how to give them optimum care.

Bamboo is not particularly fussy about soil types, and will even tolerate heavy clay soils without much decrease in vigor.

It's hard to overwater bamboo, and if you want it to grow rapidly, water deeply (with the hose on a slow trickle) once a week, and fertilize with a complete fertilizer once a month.

FERNS

There are a great many species and varieties of ferns, but the ones most common to home gardens ask similar things of soil and fertilizer.

Soil. Most ferns need a rich, well-drained soil high in organic matter. The major portion of any homemade mix should be fairly coarse peat moss, or ground bark. If you plant ferns in the ground, dig plenty of organic matter into the soil before planting.

Most ferns need a high degree of moisture both in the air (humidity) and

Boston fern

in the soil. In order not to rot roots, a well-drained soil is a necessity.

Fertilizer. Ferns are among the most tender plants grown and can be easily damaged with fertilizers, especially those high in nitrogen. Even the recommended rate on commercial formulas may be too strong. The best results are had with weak dilutions (half the recommended rate or less) of organic-based fertilizers —blood meal and fish emulsion are both good.

Heather hybrid

HEATHS AND HEATHERS

There are many, many varieties of heaths and heathers but the vast ma-

jority of them have similar soil, water and fertilizer requirements.

A soil that is made slightly acid with the addition of quantities of peat moss will suit all but a few varieties. In addition to contributing to the acidity of the soil, peat moss will improve drainage: heaths and heathers prefer a well-drained soil that is never allowed to dry out fully. As with other plants having similar requirements, a mulch of organic material will help in growing heaths and heathers. They are not heavy feeders; *infrequent* applications of a fertilizer that is acid in reaction is generally the rule.

Holly

HOLLY *(Ilex)*

Hollies are somewhat particular about the soil they are grown in. The best bet is a rich garden soil, slightly on the acid side, with good drainage. A thick, organic mulch around the root zone suits hollies just fine.

PINES

Pines are one of the few plants content to say "no" to extra helpings of organic matter, fertilizer, water and general fussing-over by gardeners. Their only real requirement is a soil that drains well. They'll do fine in soils of low fertility and they object to over-watering. The best advice is to plant them in well-drained soil and let them grow their own way.

Aleppo pine

WILLOWS

There are many willows, ranging from pussywillow *(Salix discolor)* to the common weeping willow *(S. babylonica),* and the vast majority of them are similar in one requirement: their need of large quantities of water. Many willows grow naturally near rivers, streams, lakes and ponds, and will tolerate poorly drained soils in the home garden. Willows are not particular about soil type or fertility, but remember their need for water produces a root system that can only be described as invasive.

Salix babylonica

Lawns

In these pages we'll take you from a bare patch of ground to the first mowing of a new lawn, and beyond. If you follow the procedure—even if it seems like extra work—you can be fairly certain that you'll have something worthwhile to mow.

Whether you start a lawn from seeds, sod or sprigs (plugs), the basic and important steps of soil preparation stay the same.

Soil Preparation

The drawings on page 97 assume that you are starting with a reasonably level place for planting a lawn. If not, you may have a big leveling job facing you; it might be a good idea to call in a professional with grading equipment for this initial step. The important thing is to grade the soil so that the lawn will slope slightly (and drain well) away from the house. If the lawn area has been cut up by utility lines or other trenches, fill them in with soil and soak to settle them.

An important step is shown in the first illustration—improving the soil structure with the addition of organic matter. Use whatever local sources have to offer—peat moss, ground bark, leaf mold, sawdust, rice hulls, or any number of other organic by-products that you know have not been contaminated with chemicals. Any of the above materials will add bulk to the soil and insure space for the air that is so vital for grass roots. Organic matter improves soil drainage and at the same time it holds plenty of water during hot weather. It's your best insurance against soil becoming compacted a few years down the road. Use it generously. The top 6 to 8 inches of soil should be 30 percent organic by volume. This means a 2-inch layer of organic amendment mixed in thoroughly to a depth of 6 to 8 inches.

A new lawn is in delicate condition—at least until the time for the first mowing. When grass seed germinates, the primary roots penetrate the soil to a depth of 6 to 8 inches, and they are the sole gatherers of water and nutri-

For a complete guide to lawn care, see ORTHO's *All About Lawns*.

Planting a lawn

1. Pile on organic matter—peat moss, sawdust, or whatever's available. Don't scrimp. Make 2 or 3-inch layer. Adding organic matter increases the water-holding capacity of sandy soils; and it helps open up tightly compacted clay soils.

2. Spread on 5 to 10 pounds of lawn food per 1000 square feet of lawn. This will carry lawn past first mowing. If you live where lime is used, have soil tested. Add lime for bluegrass if soil has pH below 6.0 (below natural range).

3. Till the soil, working organic matter, food, lime into the top 6 inches of soil. Go back and forth until all are blended. If organic matter hasn't been added, go easily on rototilling and rolling (the next step)—to avoid pulverizing and packing down soil.

4. Roll. Heavy roller takes out air pockets, smooths lumps. Shovel high spots into low. Roll one way, then across. If organic matter wasn't added as the first step and if the soil lacks natural humus, forget the heavy roller.

5. Level. Pick out stones, sticks, other debris. Use T-board or rake to get area to final grade. Break up clods. Scrape high

spots into low ones. Make sure finished slope conforms to grade you've planned.

6. Final rolling. If you moved much soil to fill low spots during final grading and level, roll again for the last time before planting. Use an empty roller and go in two directions. If low spots still appear, rake and roll some more.

7. Seeding. Broadcast seeds accurately with a "Whirlybird" or spreader. Rake in. Just barely cover with mulch. Roll with an empty roller.

Keep moist.

8. Sodding. Lay strips straight with ends staggered. Firm joints together by pressing with hands. Cut strips to fit corners. Roll lightly. Water to 8 inches.

9. Sprigging. For running grasses like Bermuda, lay sprigs (pieces of stems) 3 to 6-inches apart, in rows a foot apart. Cover with soil, but leave tips out. Roll.

10. Mowing. How soon the first mowing comes depends on the type of grass and the season. Generally wait until the grass grows about 2 inches tall and starts to curve. Then set mower at 1½ inches. Mow when grass is dry.

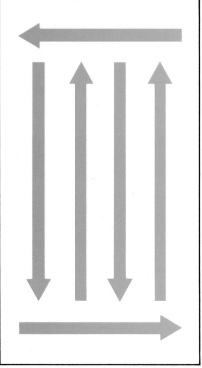

The best pattern for spreading fertilizer with a drop spreader is illustrated above. First, go along the ends, then back and forth.

ents during the first weeks of growth. Not until 1 to 4 weeks after germination do the more fibrous, secondary roots begin to develop. Because of the limited root system, don't slack off on watering until the seedlings are an inch tall. Don't walk on a brand new lawn; if you must, first lay down a plank to walk on. And don't mow or kill weeds until the time recommended on the labels of specific herbicide products: new grass is a tender plant.

Watering is especially critical and a little bit tricky in the early stages of a seeded lawn. Once seeds sprout they need moisture constantly to continue growing. Don't let them ever dry out. That may take three or more light sprinklings a day in hot weather. But, on the other hand, don't overdo it. Turn off the water before puddles can form and the runoff can carry seeds to low spots. Use sprinklers or a hose nozzle with a fine spray, particularly on sloping lawns where runoff is even more likely.

When is the best time to sow a new lawn? Spring just seems right but here are a couple of considerations. Except for some of the heat-loving grasses of the South and California, late summer

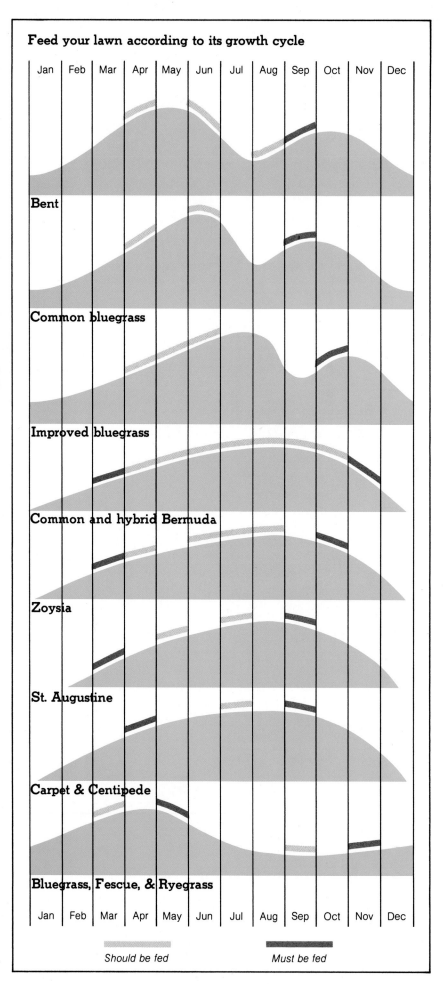

Feed your lawn according to its growth cycle

Jan | Feb | Mar | Apr | May | Jun | Jul | Aug | Sep | Oct | Nov | Dec

Bent

Common bluegrass

Improved bluegrass

Common and hybrid Bermuda

Zoysia

St. Augustine

Carpet & Centipede

Bluegrass, Fescue, & Ryegrass

Jan | Feb | Mar | Apr | May | Jun | Jul | Aug | Sep | Oct | Nov | Dec

Should be fed   *Must be fed*

or fall is a far better time. Weeds offer less competition in the fall. A new fall lawn won't have to face summer heat so early in its tender life. And it takes less water to sprout seeds in the fall than it does during the hot days of summer.

If you water your lawn regularly and it just doesn't respond, the problem may be the compaction we mentioned earlier. Compaction is especially likely in soils of fine-textured clay and can be very bad in loamy sands, as well. Foot traffic, heavy play, or movement of heavy equipment on a lawn—especially a wet lawn—can pack down soil so tightly that water, air and nutrients have a hard time getting through. As a result, the root system becomes shallow and the grass loses quality and vigor.

Compacted soils must be opened up, somehow. The best way is to rent a power aerating machine. These machines actually lift small plugs of soil and drop them on the lawn. Rake up the plugs, then spread peat moss or other organic material and fertilizer on top of the lawn, and rake into the holes. A good watering should follow this procedure to carry the nutrients and organic matter to the root zone.

If the compacted area is small, you can do a good enough job of aerating with a garden fork.

The best time to aerate a lawn is when the grass is growing actively, in spring or early fall.

Fertilizer

By far the most important element to the lawn—and the one most often in short supply—is nitrogen. Watering flushes it from the soil and the growing plant needs a plentiful and continuous supply. Without nitrogen, growth stops and the lawn becomes pale and yellowish.

Phosphorus is the next most important element for a lawn's growth, especially strong root growth. Phosphorus is particularly essential to the proper development of new plantings. It is not readily flushed from the soil by watering so most balanced lawn fertilizers have only a low percentage of phosphorus.

Potassium is the third element of critical importance to a lawn. Potassium will leach from the soil, but not as quickly as nitrogen; thus it is not needed in as great a supply. Most lawn fertilizers will supply about a third as much potassium as nitrogen but twice as much as phosphorus. Potassium is very important to winter hardiness of lawn grasses.

Of the elements needed in only tiny amounts, called micronutrients, iron is the one most often added in lawn fertilizers. If your lawn does not green up with an application of nitrogen, the problem is most likely a shortage of iron. A soil test will give you some idea of the quantity of these elements that can be supplied by your native soil.

Kinds and amounts of fertilizer

Experiments have shown that a ratio of about 5 or 6-1-2 is good for home lawns. A typical lawn fertilizer close to this ratio may have a 24-4-8 formula. It's not critical to use exactly this formula but something near it is best.

The directions on the bag will usually tell what amount to apply, or you can use our chart. Colorado state law prohibits a manufacturer from recommending less than 1 pound of actual nitrogen per 1,000 square feet at one application. Many manufacturers follow that basic guideline.

When to fertilize

Few gardeners need to be reminded to feed their lawns in spring. It helps a lawn get a head start in the battle against pests and weeds, and against the heat that's soon to come.

By midsummer, heat and light intensity slow down the growth of the cool season grasses. They usually remain green but are essentially dormant. We recommend no feeding of the cool season grasses in the summer.

The most important time to fertilize is in the fall. Fall fertilization keeps the grass growing green into cold weather. The lawn is stimulated to become more dense, and cold hardiness is improved. Not much top growth takes place in fall, so a lawn can store food that will get it off to a fast start next spring.

Some of the improved bluegrasses and Bermuda grasses need up to 50 percent more fertilizer than the common types. Give them an extra feeding in the spring and again in the fall.

Growth of the warm season grasses peaks in midsummer, then tapers off in the fall but continues until frost. The first sign of spring green comes when the soil is still cold. It is then that lawn food with quick-acting forms of nitrogen pay off, making a grass fully green sooner.

The other most important time to feed the warm season grasses comes in late fall. This keeps them growing and green as long into cold weather as possible, strengthens them against winter's cold and promotes earlier spring green-up.

Nitrogen fertilizer requirements of specific grasses

Pounds per year per 1,000 square feet	Warm Season Grasses	Cool Season Grasses
1 to 4	Bahia Centipede	Hard fescue
2 to 6	Carpet	Chewings fescue Red fescue
4 to 10	Common Bermuda Zoysia	Annual rye grass Colonial bent grass Perennial rye grass Tall fescue
6 to 12	Hybrid Bermuda	Creeping bent grass Kentucky bluegrass

The rates show the range for grasses with a long growing season. Lower rates would apply in northern and eastern areas with shorter growing seasons.

A Sprinkler System

A well-groomed garden, especially the lawn, deserves a sprinkler system that will distribute the right amount of water when and where it's needed. With today's easy-to-use materials and equipment, a little know-how and a couple of weekends, a handy gardener can install an effective, time- and water-saving irrigation system.

Start With a Plan

Begin your sprinkler system with graph paper (a good size is 10 grids to the inch, the inch equaling 10 feet), a soft lead pencil, an inexpensive compass and a measuring tape. A plan on paper will help you install a better system. Besides, a carefully prepared plan helps when ordering materials, makes it easier in getting advice from your garden supply center or hardware dealer, and serves to remind you where you put the pipelines.

Make your plan complete
A good plan is actually a bird's-eye view of your property drawn to scale. It should show all construction and landscape features that could affect the installation and operation of the sprinkler system. These include the obvious items shown on the sketch and checklist, and less apparent objects such as a mail box, raised planters and buried drainage or electrical lines. If significant, it also is helpful to note prevailing wind direction, sun/shade areas, and steep slopes as well as high and low spots in your landscape. Water-sensitive plants also should be noted.

Planning the plumbing
A sprinkler system is essentially an assembly of pipe (copper, galvanized or plastic), pipe fittings, valves and sprinkler heads connected to a water source. Its three essentials are (1) good design, (2) quality materials and equipment that fit the design and (3) careful installation.

Modern materials make it easy
Space does not allow comparison of the various piping materials and sprinkler equipment now on the market. But the materials and methods suggested here lend themselves to easy, economical and efficient installation.

Pipe and fittings
A ¾-inch copper or galvanized iron water-service line usually requires a sprinkler main to the valve assembly of the same size and material. However, if static water pressure is low—say, under 40 pounds per square inch (psi)—or if the distance from the meter to the sprinkler valves is more than 50 feet, or if the service line is partially clogged, then the use of 1-inch pipe is recommended. Your local water company can help you at this stage. (See Typical Connection Chart, page 101.)

PVC (polyvinyl chloride) plastic.
Ease of handling and assembly, durability, outstanding flow characteristics, low cost and ready availability, and easy repairs recommend PVC pipe and solvent-welded fittings as the ideal plastic for sprinkler installations where building codes permit its use. PVC normally is sold in 20-foot lengths and usually colored white or gray. Nominal ½-inch PVC pipe, commonly used for residential installations, has an actual inside diameter of 0.622 inch. The nominal ¾-inch, used for feeder lines, has an inside diameter of 0.824 inch.

Sprinkler valves.
Angle valves are used for shrubbery heads installed above ground level. For lawn sprinkler heads installed at ground level, anti-syphon valves are recommended (and usually required by local plumbing codes) to prevent accidental backflow. Angle valves are installed underground, whereas anti-syphon valves should be placed 6 inches or more above ground level. Typically, valve sizes are ¾ or 1 inch, matching the pipe size of the sprinkler main. In cold winter areas, drain valves at the end of runs and at the major hookup to the house main are necessary to prevent frozen pipes, valves and fittings. Automatic drain valves make the job easier, but may require checking to be sure they function properly.

Sprinkler heads.
While a wide variety of sprinkler heads is available for every conceivable application, most residential lawns and gardens can best be served by using matched, adjustable, pop-up lawn sprinkler heads and shrubbery heads with full, half-circle or quarter-circle spray patterns. It is important to remember that each sprinkler head is designed to discharge a specified number of gallons per minute (gpm) over a given radius, and that each head requires a certain water pressure in order for it to achieve its maximum throw. Plan and purchase wisely: you can easily reduce the radius but you cannot stretch the coverage of any sprinkler head beyond its capacity.

Take your time. In planning the plumbing, check on codes and permits. Find out from your local water company the size of your meter, static water pressure, and expected pressure fluctuations—between summer and winter, morning and afternoon, or other periods. Visit your hardware dealer or garden center to talk about materials and costs.

Plan the entire plumbing system. Even though your immediate project calls for doing just the front garden, think about running a sprinkler main (often one size larger) to the back yard. Or you may at least want to install a tie-in fitting for possible future use. A

Check List

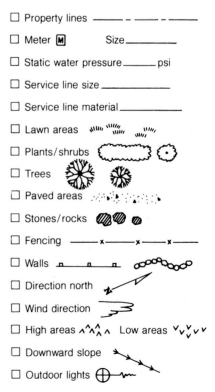

☐ Property lines

☐ Meter M   Size_____

☐ Static water pressure_____ psi

☐ Service line size_____

☐ Service line material_____

☐ Lawn areas

☐ Plants/shrubs

☐ Trees

☐ Paved areas

☐ Stones/rocks

☐ Fencing

☐ Walls

☐ Direction north

☐ Wind direction

☐ High areas   Low areas

☐ Downward slope

☐ Outdoor lights

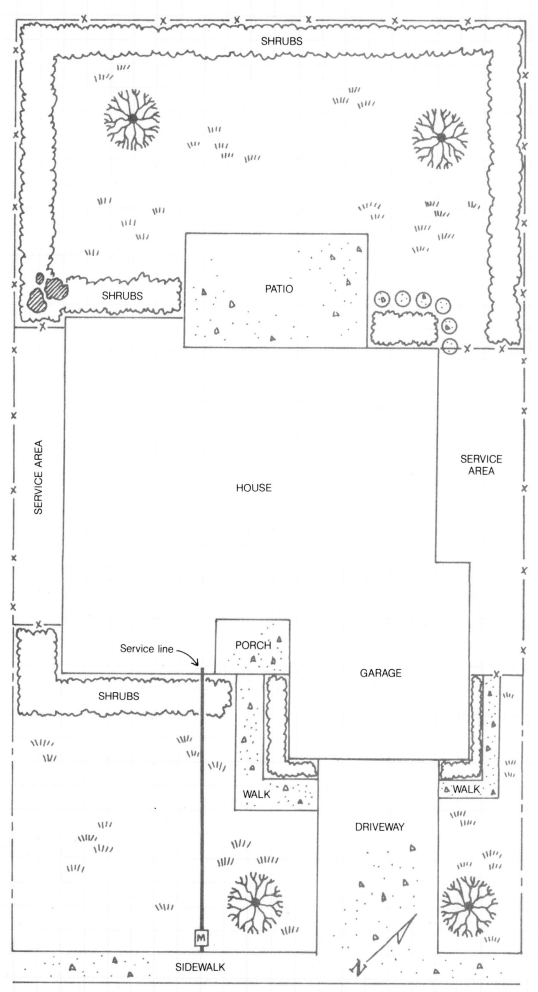

SHRUBS

SHRUBS

PATIO

SERVICE AREA

SERVICE AREA

HOUSE

Service line

PORCH

GARAGE

SHRUBS

WALK

WALK

DRIVEWAY

M

SIDEWALK

Please Note:
If your home is on a hilltop; gets its water from wells; has under-size or outdated plumbing; or otherwise has low water pressure and volume, professional advice is recommended. The information presented here is intended as a guide for typical installations.

Typical valve assembly

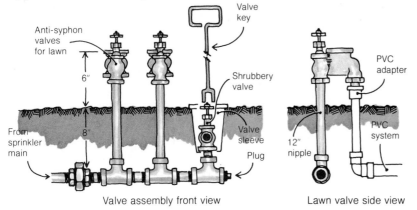

Anti-syphon valves for lawn

Valve key

Shrubbery valve

6"

8"

From sprinkler main

Valve sleeve

Plug

PVC adapter

PVC system

12" nipple

Valve assembly front view

Lawn valve side view

Sprinkler heads

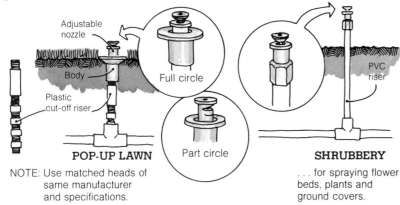

Adjustable nozzle

Body

Plastic cut-off riser

Full circle

PVC riser

POP-UP LAWN

Part circle

SHRUBBERY

NOTE: Use matched heads of same manufacturer and specifications.

. . . for spraying flower beds, plants and ground covers.

tee with a plug or cap (rather than an elbow) can save a lot of work later on.

Locating the valves. Plumbing in the garden is seldom attractive, so valves should be inconspicuous but readily accessible. Be sure, too, that valves can be turned on and off without your getting wet.

Sizing the pipe. When it comes to sprinkler systems, a trickle of water through a 12-inch pipe is about as useless as a high-pressure jet of water from a pinhole. Adequate volume (gpm) and pressure (psi) go hand in hand and where pressure is marginal, use the next larger size of pipe to reduce friction loss and thus pressure drop.

Special plumbing problems. These need not slow you down. Cold country systems require inexpensive drain valves set at various low points in the sprinkler lines. Where there is a pressure reducer valve, cut in ahead of it to take advantage of the higher pressure. If your service line runs up a hill, this will reduce your static water pressure about a half-pound for each foot of rise.

Pipe fittings

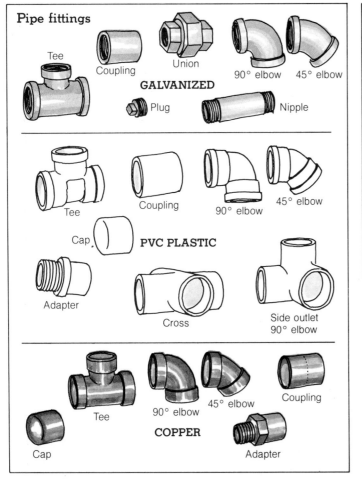

Tee

Coupling

Union

90° elbow

45° elbow

GALVANIZED

Plug

Nipple

Tee

Coupling

90° elbow

45° elbow

Cap

PVC PLASTIC

Adapter

Cross

Side outlet 90° elbow

Tee

90° elbow

45° elbow

Coupling

COPPER

Cap

Adapter

Pop-up lawn and shrubbery sprinkler heads
(typical performance table*)

Spray Pattern	STANDARD HEADS			
	Coverage	gpm Discharge	Maximum Spacing	
FULL	24' dia.	4.0	17'	15'
HALF	12' rad.	2.5		
QUARTER	12' rad.	1.8		

Spray Pattern	UNDERSIZE HEADS			
	Coverage	gpm Discharge	Maximum Spacing	
FULL	20' dia.	2.0	14'	12'
HALF	10' rad.	1.5		
QUARTER	10' rad.	1.0		

*Based on recommended pressure at each sprinkler head.

NOTE: Use of undersize sprinkler heads is recommended for low pressure/volume installations.

A typical situation

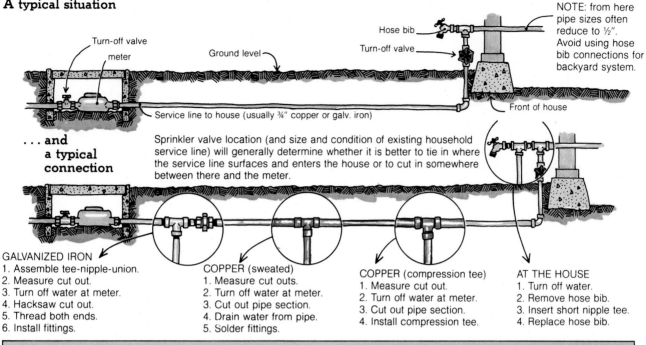

NOTE: from here pipe sizes often reduce to ½". Avoid using hose bib connections for backyard system.

Turn-off valve
meter
Ground level
Hose bib
Turn-off valve
Front of house
Service line to house (usually ¾" copper or galv. iron)

...and a typical connection

Sprinkler valve location (and size and condition of existing household service line) will generally determine whether it is better to tie in where the service line surfaces and enters the house or to cut in somewhere between there and the meter.

GALVANIZED IRON
1. Assemble tee-nipple-union.
2. Measure cut out.
3. Turn off water at meter.
4. Hacksaw cut out.
5. Thread both ends.
6. Install fittings.

COPPER (sweated)
1. Measure cut outs.
2. Turn off water at meter.
3. Cut out pipe section.
4. Drain water from pipe.
5. Solder fittings.

COPPER (compression tee)
1. Measure cut out.
2. Turn off water at meter.
3. Cut out pipe section.
4. Install compression tee.

AT THE HOUSE
1. Turn off water.
2. Remove hose bib.
3. Insert short nipple tee.
4. Replace hose bib.

Maximum gallons per minute (gpm) allowable for each sprinkler valve grouping

Length of Supply lines	Sizes of:				Static water pressure (psi)					
	Water meter	Supply lines	Sprinkler		30	40	50	60	70	80
			Valve	PVC Pipe	Gallons per minute (gpm)					
50 ft. max.	¾"	¾"	¾"	½"	6	9	12	14	16	18
	¾"	1"	1"	¾"	10	13	17	19	23	26
100 ft. max.	¾"	¾"	¾"	½"	5	7	9	12	13	15
	¾"	1"	1"	¾"	7	12	15	18	20	23

NOTE: Supply lines should include applicable length of service line and sprinkler main.

Grouping the heads

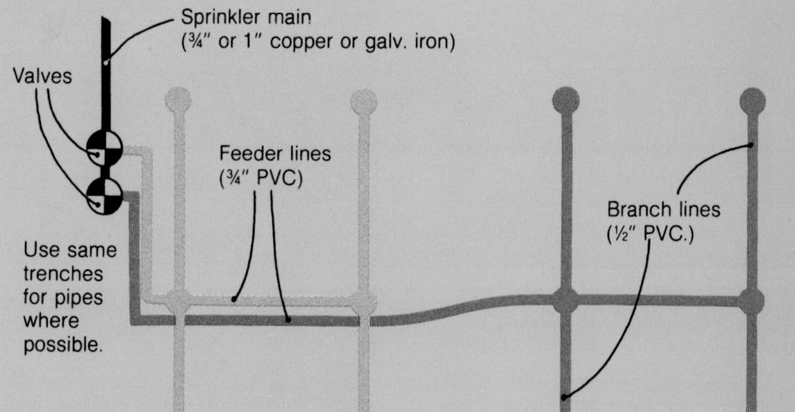

Sprinkler main (¾" or 1" copper or galv. iron)
Valves
Feeder lines (¾" PVC)
Branch lines (½" PVC.)
Use same trenches for pipes where possible.

Splitting the flow

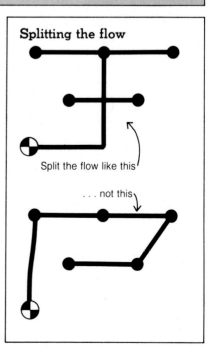

Split the flow like this
. . . not this

Working with PVC

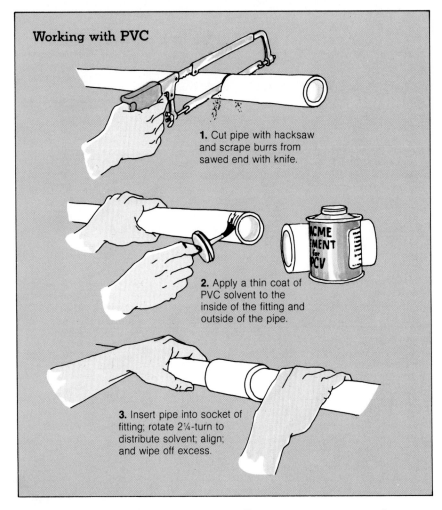

1. Cut pipe with hacksaw and scrape burrs from sawed end with knife.

2. Apply a thin coat of PVC solvent to the inside of the fitting and outside of the pipe.

3. Insert pipe into socket of fitting; rotate 2¼-turn to distribute solvent; align; and wipe off excess.

Good design is worth the time. When you have decided what your plumbing to the valves should look like, it's time to get out the compass. Let's assume you have decided to use small lawn pop-up sprinkler heads whose maximum coverage is a radius of 10 feet and recommended triangular spacing pattern is 14 feet—or a 12-foot radius on a square pattern.

Set your compass to a 10-foot radius on your scale drawing. Lightly draw in quarter circles wherever a 90 degree angle is shown within the area to be sprinkled. Next, draw the half circles normally located adjacent to paved areas, buildings and property lines. Finally, fill in the center areas using full circles. Show the full-, half- and quarter-circles with symbols.

Here are a few good rules to follow:
—Overlap the outer third of a sprinkler head's spray radius.
—Cut back the radius of your circles to accommodate design but do not attempt to stretch it.

—Design your system so that water is sprayed from the outside perimeter inward toward the center.
—Experiment with various full- and part-circle combinations and spacing patterns of heads until coverage is complete, with no potential dry spots.
—Plan to water lawns and planted areas separately unless the plants are hardy or the sprinkler heads can be placed to deliver optimum amounts of water to the plants.

Grouping the heads. To determine the number of valves required and which valve will operate what heads, you will need to know the gpm requirement for each sprinkler head, and the total gallonage requirement for the whole system. By determining from the chart (page 101) the number of gallons you can flow through your system at any one time, you can easily find out the number of valves you will need.

Next, the sprinkler heads should be grouped in such a way that no grouping exceeds the allowable gallonage.

The plan comes to life

STEP 1
Install Valve System
- Assemble valve assembly with PVC adapters in advance.
- Cut-in tee for sprinkler main.
- Dig trench to valves.
- Install & flush valves.
- Check for leaks.

STEP 2
Stake Layout
- Use stakes and string to mark sprinkler heads and pipe trench locations.

STEP 3
Dig Trenches
- Use a flat edged spade to dig v-shaped trenches (5" wide at the top and 6-8" deep).

STEP 4
Assemble PVC pipe
- Solvent-weld PVC pipe and fittings.
- Wait 12 hours.
- Insert plastic risers.
- Flush out pipe lines.
- Install sprinkler heads.

STEP 5
Test for Coverage
- Turn on each valve and be sure entire area is covered properly.
- Lower pop-up heads to proper level.

STEP 6
Backfill Trenches
- Fill trench a little higher than bottom of sod.
- Replace sod.
- Tamp to proper level using a brick.

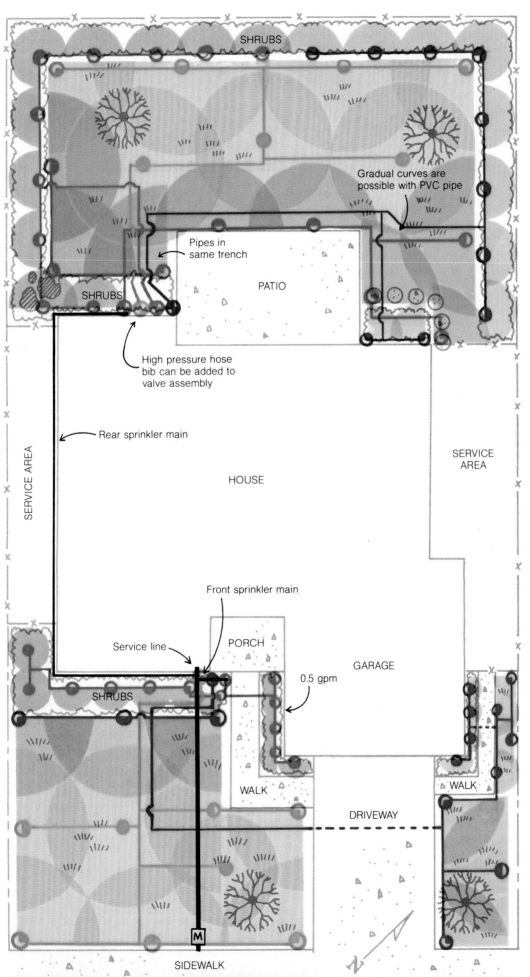

SHRUBS

Gradual curves are possible with PVC pipe

Pipes in same trench

PATIO

SHRUBS

High pressure hose bib can be added to valve assembly

SERVICE AREA

Rear sprinkler main

SERVICE AREA

HOUSE

Front sprinkler main

Service line

PORCH

GARAGE

0.5 gpm

SHRUBS

WALK

WALK

DRIVEWAY

M

SIDEWALK

The completed plan shows that it is possible to water the entire garden, front and back, automatically. It isn't necessary to install the entire system at once, but if you install it in stages, be sure to start with a long-range master plan.

A Gardener's Glossary

Acid, alkaline or neutral soil reaction. The pH of most soils is between 4.5 and 8.0.

High rainfall areas tend to have acid soils—in practical terms, soils with pH below 6.0. Light rainfall areas tend to have alkaline soils—again in practical terms, soils with pH above 7.3.

Agricultural lime is useful for correcting a very acid soil (about 5 lb. of ground limestone per 100 sq. ft. every 5 years).

Alkalinity in soils is reduced by the application of iron sulfate, aluminum sulfate or large amounts of sawdust, peat moss or ground bark.

Acre. A land area containing 43,560 square feet and measuring, for example, approximately 210 x 210 feet.

Actual. That part of a product's formula that refers to specific ingredients. For example, a 5 lb. box of a general-purpose plant food 10-10-10 would have 10% nitrogen, 10% phosphate and 10% potash. 10% of 5 lb. is ½ pound. Therefore, the *actual* content of the three major ingredients in the 5 lb. box is ½ pound each.

Aeration of soil. The exchange of air in the soil with air from the atmosphere. The composition of the air in a well-aerated soil is similar to that in the atmosphere; in a poorly aerated soil the problem may be not enough air, as in flooded soils, compacted soils, etc. In these cases, the air is considerably higher in carbon dioxide and lower in oxygen than the atmosphere above the soil.

Agricultural extension agent. See Extension Service.

Amendment. Any material, such as lime, gypsum, sawdust or synthetic conditioners that is worked into the soil to change the soil characteristics. Strictly speaking, a fertilizer is also an amendment, but the term "amendment" is used most commonly for added material other than fertilizer.

Ammonia. A colorless gas composed of one atom of nitrogen and three atoms of hydrogen. Ammonia liquefied under pressure is used commercially as a fertilizer, and as the basis for many home-garden fertilizers.

Annual plant. A plant living one year or less. During this time the plant grows, blooms, produces seeds and dies. Examples are beans, sweet corn, cucumber, melon, marigolds, zinnias.

Auxin. A plant hormone that influences and regulates plant growth.

Available nutrient. The part of the supply of a plant nutrient when applied in the soil that can be taken up by plants at rates and in amounts significant to plant growth.

Available water. The part of water in the soil that can be taken up by plants usable; obtainable.

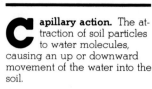

Ball (including Balled and Burlapped). Ball refers to soil encasing roots of plants being transplanted or shipped. The ball of soil around the roots, which keeps them from being disturbed, is often bound in burlap or similar mesh material. (Abbreviated "B and B.")

Ball

Banding (*of fertilizers*). The placement of fertilizers in the soil in narrow bands, usually at specific distances from the row of seeds or plants. The fertilizer bands are covered by soil but are not mixed with it.

Bare root. In the wintertime or in early spring, many varieties of deciduous plants are sold with their roots bare. Dormant plants, dug from the soil, have their roots cleaned and trimmed, and are prevented from drying out until the time they should be planted.

Basin irrigation. The application of irrigation water to level areas that are surrounded by border ridges or levees.

Bedrock. The solid rock underlying soils and other earthy surface formations.

Biennial plant. A plant that completes its normal term of life in two years by flowering and fruiting in the second year.

Biodegradable. Any material that can readily be decomposed in the soil by the action of microorganisms.

Broadcasting. Scattering a material such as fertilizer or seed evenly over a soil surface.

Buffer, buffering (*of soil*). The clay, organic matter, and compounds such as carbonates that enable soil to resist appreciable changes in pH.

Capillary action. The attraction of soil particles to water molecules, causing an up or downward movement of the water into the soil.

Cation. An atom that is electrically charged as the result of the loss of electrons. The common soil cations are calcium, magnesium, sodium, ammonium, potassium and hydrogen.

Chelate (*ke'late*). Several of the micronutrients such as iron may be prevalent in the soil but unavailable to the plant because they're locked into insoluble compounds. When a chelating agent with the micronutrient is added, the nutrient element is made available to the plant.

Chlorophyll. The green photosynthetic coloring matter found in plants, particularly in the leaves, where it is continually being manufactured. Known to have a vital role in converting carbon dioxide and water into simple sugars by the process of photosynthesis.

Chlorosis. Lack of green in a leaf, caused by nutritional failure or disease. It is frequently caused by lack of a plant's ability to take up iron. In severe cases the entire leaf except the veins turns yellow. Often there is enough iron in the soil, but it's not available to the plant. Lowering the soil pH or using a chelate with iron will help correct most chlorotic conditions.

Chlorosis

Clay. Mineral soil particles less than 0.002 millimeters in diameter. As a soil class, soil material that contains 40% or more clay, less than 45% sand and less than 40% silt.

Clone. A group of organisms derived from a single individual by asexual reproduction.

Compost. A decomposing mixture of vegetable matter. Gardeners usually build a compost with alternating layers of the vegetable matter and fertilized soil.

Contour planting. Horizontal planting in rows that follow the contours of a slope or grade to better control water drainage

and erosion of soil.

Contour planting

Controlled-release fertilizers. Release their nutrients in regulated amounts. These are (1) slightly soluble fertilizers that slowly dissolve in the soil, (2) plastic-coated fertilizers through which water slowly penetrates to release the soluble content.

Cover crop. Sometimes referred to as "green manure," a cover crop is useful in large gardens where some of the soil lies dormant in winter. Any of the legumes (alfalfa, clover, cow peas, etc.) sown in fall and turned over in early spring will return valuable humus and nitrogen to soil.

Crop rotation. Maintaining the good condition of a given section of soil by alternate planting of different crops. Such planting also helps to discourage insects that thrive on a given crop and diseases indigenous to a certain kind of plant.

Cultivation. The loosening of a soil with either a hand- or mechanical-type implement chiefly for the purpose of controlling weeds.

Culture. A specialized activity used in growing plants (e.g., pruning, cultivation, watering).

Damping off. A plant disease caused by certain fungus in the soil. Seedlings die immediately before or just after they break through the soil. Careful watering, good drainage and disinfecting seedbed soil help in preventing damping off.

Deciduous. A plant that sheds all its leaves at one time once a year.

Deep rooted. Plants with deeply-growing roots as distinct from plants with roots growing on or close to the surface.

Denitrification. The process by which nitrates or nitrites in the soil or organic deposits are reduced to lower oxides, by bacterial action, to free nitrogen or ammonia.

Dew. Condensed moisture from the atmosphere adhering in the form of small drops to any cool surface.

Dew point. A temperature point below which moisture in the atmosphere is condensed into small drops.

Dibble or dibber. A handheld pointed tool for making holes in the soil for planting seeds, bulbs, transplants, etc.

Dormancy. Cyclic period when a plant rests and its growth processes greatly slow down. This occurs in many species with the coming of winter as days grow shorter and temperatures begin to drop. The period ends in spring when the plant is exposed to higher temperatures for an extended number of hours. Dormancy is a plant's safeguard against extremes of temperature, etc.

Drainage *(air).* A term used to describe the circulation of air (oxygen) into the soil and the flow of respiration product (mostly carbon dioxide) out of the soil. Compacted soil around roots resists air flow, making it difficult for many plants to thrive. Also refers to movement of air from adjacent areas that affects temperature for sensitive, growing crops such as citrus.

Drainage *(water).* A term used to describe how water passes through root areas of plants. This passage is essential to the proper growth of almost all plants.

Drill. A tiny furrow made with the corner of hoe or pointed stick, a bit deeper than the seed to be planted. All vegetables grown from seeds planted in straight rows are sown in drills. Also, an implement used in seeding.

Drill

Drip irrigation. A system for watering at points on or just below the soil surface so that only small areas are moistened by slowly dripping water. The irrigation is made with very low water pressure using a small emitter.

Drip line. A line drawn around a tree directly under the outer-most ends of its branches — the point at which rain water drips off.

Drip Line

Drought. A period of dryness, especially a long one. Usually considered to be any period of soil moisture deficiency within the plant root zone. A period of dryness of sufficient length to deplete soil moisture to the extent that plant growth is seriously retarded.

Dry-off. A method often used to help a plant or bulb enter dormancy or a rest period in good condition by gradually reducing the amount of water it normally receives.

Early-maturing. A descriptive term applied to certain vegetables that mature faster than others of the same species; i.e., a faster growing variety.

Ecology. The study of living things in their environment and the interdependence between all forms of life and their natural habitats.

Environment. The complete surroundings of an organism or an ecological community.

Enzymes. Substances produced by living cells which can bring about or speed up chemical reaction. They are organic catalysts.

Erosion. The wearing away of the land surface by detachment and transport of soil and rock materials through the action of moving water or wind, or geological agents.

Exotic. Plants that are introduced to a region other than that to which they are considered native.

Extension service. A function of the Federal, State and County Cooperative Extension system that provides agricultural and home economics information to residents of the states. Each state has a Land Grant University conducting research and providing educational publications. Most counties have an extension agent, and many have gardening information for distribution.

Fallow. Cropland left idle in order to restore productivity, mainly through the accumulation of water, nutrients or both.

Fertilizer. A material that provides one or more essential nutrients in forms that can be used by growing plants. The term generally refers to materials of organic or inorganic origin that are known to increase nitrogen, phosphate and potash when added to soil or dissolved in water.

Fibrous root system. Made up of many branched roots and rootlets (sometimes with no taproot development), as distinguished from bulbous or tuberous roots.

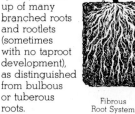

Fibrous Root System

Field capacity. The amount of moisture remaining in a soil 2 or 3 days after having been saturated and after free drainage has practically ceased.

Fill. Soil or other materials used to change the elevation or level the grade of an area.

Fixation. The conversion of a soluble material, such as a plant nutrient like phosphorous, from a soluble or exchangeable form to a relatively insoluble form.

Flat. A single shallow box or tray used to start cuttings or seedlings.

Flower. Usually a symmetrical form of colorful growth whose primary purpose is to produce seed for subsequent reproduction. The seed-bearing plant's reproductive organ.

Foliage plant. Plant grown especially for the beauty of leaves or foliage as contrasted to a plant grown for flowers or fruit.

Foliar feeding. The process of providing mineral nutrients to plant foliage and stems with soluble fertilizers.

Frost. Temperature below the dew point, causing freezing condition and a covering of minute ice particles on exposed objects.

Fumigation. Applying chemicals or gases to control insects, diseases, and weeds within an enclosed area or under a plastic cover.

Fungi. Forms of plant life that lack chlorophyll and are unable to make their own food. Includes both beneficial and pathological forms.

Fungicide. A chemical material used to retard or prevent the growth of fungi.

Furrow. A small ditch (often V-shaped) made for deep seed planting or irrigating.

Genus. The class of a related group of plants, each consisting of one or more species.

Germination. The sprouting of a seed and the commencement of growth. (Also used to mean the starting of plants from seeds.)

Grading. Modifying a ground area by cutting or filling to make it level.

Granular fertilizer. A fertilizer composed of particles of roughly similar size, usually about 1/10 inch in diameter.

Green manure. A cover crop that is turned under while still green. (See Cover crop.)

Ground cover. Refers to both plants and inert material used to cover certain areas for the purpose of preventing soil erosion or to discourage the intrusion of undesirable plants. Also used as an ornamental in landscape design.

Growing medium. Specially formulated soil substitute prepared for plant growing.

Growing season. The period of time from the last plant-killing frost in the spring to the first plant-killing frost in the fall.

Growth regulators. Any synthetic or natural organic compound—such as indoleacetic acid, gibberellin, abcissic acid, 2,4-D, naphthalene acetic acid —that in dilute amounts will promote, inhibit or modify plant growth processes. Also called auxins, plant hormones and phytohormones. These hormones regulate leaf drop, root initiation, bud dormancy, bending of plants in response to light, etc.

Hardening. A process of slowing plant growth by withholding water, lowering the temperature, decreasing fertilizer or gradually shifting the plants from a more sheltered environment to a less sheltered environment. The process of hardening plants is used to increase chances for survival at transplanting time.

Hardpan. A hardened or naturally-cemented soil horizon or layer. The soil material may be sandy or clayey and may be cemented by iron oxide, silica, calcium carbonate or other substances.

Hardy plant. A plant that can be planted before the last killing frost in the spring. The word hardy applied to plants means the ability to resist frost.

Heaving. Occurs in winter as a result of alternate freezing and thawing. The soil cracks and lifts, often thrusting small plants out of the soil and damaging their roots. (May be at least partially counteracted by deep planting or by the application of a mulch to protect from freezing.)

Heavy soil. An old term formerly used for clayey or fine-textured soils. The term originated from the heavy draught on the horses when plowing this soil.

Heeling in. A method for storing plants temporarily by burying or covering their roots with materials such as sawdust or soil.

Heeling In

Herbaceous plant. A plant described as having a soft, non-woody stem. Generally, these plants live and grow for only one season. The exceptions are herbaceous perennials, which die down to their root crown, but grow new top growth each year.

Hills. In gardening terms, a group of 3 or 4 plants whose seeds, usually 7 to 10 in number, have been sown in a circle from 12 to 15 inches in diameter, evenly spaced. After the plants come up, all but 3 or 4 of the strongest are removed from the soil.

Hills

Host plant. Any plant that furnishes sustenance for a plant pest. In the literal sense, any plant that a bug or disease lives on is a host plant. In general usage, however, the term describes a plant that is notorious for offering sustenance to any one bad pest—as cabbage-family plants are host plants to harlequin plant bug; as wheat, corn and native prairie grasses are hosts to chinch bugs in the South; and as barberries are hosts to blister rust.

Hybrid. A plant resulting from interbreeding two plants of the same type that have different individual characteristics for a trait (e.g., tall or short for the height trait). Frequently the cross results in greater vigor, disease resistance, etc.

Hydroponics. The growing of plants in water (without any soil), to which plant nutrients have been added.

Impervious. Not penetrable by water or other fluids.

Indigenous. Plants native to a particular region. Opposite of exotic.

Inorganic. Substances occurring as minerals in nature or obtainable from them by chemical means.

Inorganic nitrogen. Nitrogen in combination with other elements, not in animal or vegetable form. Ammonium sulfate and calcium nitrate are examples.

Ion. An electrically charged particle. In reference to soils, an ion is an electrically charged element or compound either in solution or held by the electrostatic particles in the soil.

Irrigation. Applying water to the soil during periods when natural rainfall does not occur in enough volume to maintain a desirable level of soil moisture for plant growth.

Leaching. The removal of materials in solution by the passage of water through the soil.

Leaf mulcher. See Shredder.

Legume. A group of plants which bear legumes or pods. In some species the root system is invaded by nitrifying bacteria. These bacteria convert nitrogen into forms that can be utilized by the plant.

Lifting. The digging up of a plant that is to be replanted.

Light soil. A soil that is easy to work. Also, a coarse-textured soil such as sand.

Lime. In strict chemical terminology, lime refers to calcium oxide (CaO), but the word is now used for all limestone-derived materials applied to neutralize acid soils.

Loam. The textural class name for soil having a moderate amount of sand, silt and clay.

Long-season crop. A crop that requires a maximum of frost-free days to produce a satisfactory crop.

Luxury consumption. The intake by a plant of an essential nutrient in amounts exceeding what it needs.

Manure. Generally, the refuse from stables and barnyards, including both animal excrements and straw or other litter.

Mellow soil. A porous, softly granular soil easily worked without becoming compacted.

Metalized mulch. A film that is made with a silver or aluminum coating. This has the advantage of increased light reflection; it also works as an aphid repellant. Not readily available for the home gardener at the present time.

Microclimate. The climate of a small area or locality, particularly near the ground level—e.g., a back yard or portion of a garden—as distinct from the climate of a county or state.

Micronutrients. Nutrients that plants need in only small, trace, or minute amounts.

Microorganisms. Forms of life too small to be seen with the unaided eye, or barely discernible.

Mildew. A white, cottony coating on plants that later turns them black and wrinkled. Caused by various fungi, especially during periods of warm days and cool nights.

Mineral soil. A general term for a soil composed chiefly of mineral matter, in contrast to an organic soil that is composed chiefly of organic matter.

Mineralization. The conversion of an element from an organic form to an inorganic state as a result of microbial decomposition.

Mist. A procedure using vaporized water within an enclosed space to provide constant moisture for plant growth when propagating.

Mulch. Any material applied to the soil surface to conserve soil moisture, raise or maintain a more even soil temperature and/or aid in weed control. The mulch may be of manure, leaf mold, straw, sawdust, plastic, even paper.

Mutation. A change in a plant gene that produces an offspring differing from the parent.

Nematode. A minute, threadlike transparent worm that feeds upon living and dead organic matter. Some are parasites that infest roots, bulbs and leaves.

Neutral soil. A soil that is neither acid nor alkaline. Strictly, a neutral soil has a pH of 7.0; in practice, a neutral soil has a pH between 6.5 and 7.5.

Nitrification. The formation of nitrates and nitrites from ammonia (or ammonium compounds), as in soils by microorganisms.

Nitrogen. One of the essential nutrients needed for plant growth. It is required for all living plants and animals since it is a component of protein. If the supply of nitrogen is good, foliage is green and the plant flourishes. Insufficient nitrogen is indicated by yellowing leaves and stunted growth. Too much nitrogen may cause excessive growth, making plants more susceptible to frost and disease.

NPK. The chemical symbols for the primary nutrients needed by plants. N is for nitrogen; P is for phosphate; K is for potassium. The percent of each element in a package or bottle of fertilizer is always shown in NPK order.

Nutrient solution. Liquid containing some or all of the mineral elements required for plant growth. Especially applied to use in hydroponics.

Organic matter. A term applied to a substance containing carbon compounds and usually obtained from decomposed plant or animal material. Needed to maintain a healthy soil structure and bacterial life.

Ornamental. Mostly, plants grown for beauty of form, flower or foliage rather than for food or fruit. However, many herbs and vegetables—leeks, borage—and dwarf fruit trees are also considered ornamental.

Ortho. Prefix meaning straight, proper or correct.

Over-potting. Planting in a pot that is larger than necessary for the rootball, causing the soil to become water-saturated and poorly aerated.

Oxide. A combination of any element with oxygen alone.

Parasite. A pest or disease that lives on or within an organism of another species known as the host. The parasite obtains its nutrients from the host, which can lead to the deterioration or death of the latter.

Parts per million (ppm). A notation for indicating small amounts of materials, usually by weight. For soil it is the number of units by weight of the substance per million units of oven-dry soil (1 pound per million pounds; 1 gram per million grams, etc.). For solutions, it is the number of weight units of substance per million units of solution.

Peat. Partially decayed organic plant matter from ancient swamps used for mulching and soil improvement.

Peat pot. Made of compressed. peat (or other like material), used for the starting of plants that are to be transplanted in the pot directly into the soil.

Perennial plant. A plant that normally lives more than two years.

Perlite. A volcanic mineral expanded by heat treatment to form lightweight white granules. It is used either for soil conditioning or as a rooting medium for plants. Also used in synthetic soil formulas and as a substitute for sand in potting mixes.

Pesticide. A substance (most often a chemical) used to control weeds, fungi, insects and the like.

pH. A numerical designation indicating the relative acidity or alkalinity in soils and other biological systems. Technically, pH is the common logarithm of the reciprocal of the hydrogen-ion concentration of a solution. A pH of 7.0 indicates neutrality, higher values indicate increasing alkalinity and lower values indicate increasing acidity.

Phosphate. A compound of phosphorous. See NPK.

Photoperiod. A term applied to hours of light required daily to achieve normal maturity. Plants are often referred to as long-day plants, short-day plants, or intermediate plants. The plant's response to its photoperiod is known as photoperiodism.

Photosynthesis. The process of conversion by plants of water and carbon dioxide into carbohydrates under the action of light, chlorophyll and a living cell.

Phototropism. The growth of plants toward light in response to light stimulus.

Plant nutrient. Any element taken in by a plant that is essential to its growth and used by it in its growth processes.

Plant spacing. The distance between individual plants growing in a row.

Plastic mulch. One of the newer forms of mulching materials. Many polyethylene materials, sold under various trade names, are available either black or clear, slit or solid, in varying widths.

Pollination. The transfer of pollen from the stamens (staminate flower) to the pistils (pistillate flower). Plants are either cross-pollinating or self-pollinating. Cross-pollinating means the transfer of pollen from flowers of one plant to the flowers of another (either of the same species or a different species). Self-pollinating takes place when pollen is transferred between the reproductive organs of an individual flower or between flowers on the same plant (e.g. sweet peas).

Pomology. The science of growing fruit.

Porosity. The degree to which the soil mass is permeated with pores or cavities. Porosity can be generally expressed as that percentage of the whole volume of a soil horizon which is unoccupied by solid particles.

Potash. Potassium carbonate, often obtained from wood ashes. Also used to refer to the third of the three major plant nutrients. See NPK.

Potbound. A potted plant, the roots of which have become thickly matted, is said to be potbound. See Rootbound.

Potbound

Potting. The transplant of any plant to a single pot.

Potting mixture. A combination of various ingredients designed for growing plants in containers.

Pre-emergence. Generally, chemical treatment of soil to kill weed seeds before they germinate or after a crop is planted but before it emerges.

Primary mineral. A mineral that occurs, or originally occurred, in igneous rocks; examples are micas and feldspars.

Propagation. Reproduction of plants either from seeds (sexual reproduction) or from cuttings, division, budding, grafting or layering (asexual reproduction).

Residual fertilizer. The amount of fertilizer that remains in the soil after one or more cropping seasons.

Respiration. As applied to plants, the chemical process by which a plant absorbs oxygen, then releases energy from the oxidizing of plant sugars to water and carbon dioxide. Plant soil should be sufficiently aerated so that oxygen is able to get to the plant's roots.

Rest period. A normal period in a plant's life when it does not grow any larger. Perennials, which have an annual cycle, grow to flower or fruit during part of a year, then rest during the remainder. Even plants in a temperate climate follow this pattern. See Dormancy.

Rootbound. Undesirable condition of a plant that has grown too long in a container so that its roots have become "choked."

Root crop. The term used to describe crops grown for edible roots, e.g. beets, carrots, turnips.

Root pruning. A method for fostering the development of a branched root system, helpful in transplanting or as a method of invigorating the plant.

Root Pruning

Row. Generally speaking, planted by drill method (see Drill). An exception is planting peas, where seeds are scattered.

Row spacing. Distance between plant rows.

Runner. A long, thin, trailing stem that develops new plants when the nodes contact the soil, e.g., strawberry runner.

Rust. A fungus that infects garden plants such as roses. Characterized by round pustules filled with reddish or yellow spores on on the leaves.

Saline soil. A soil containing enough soluble salts to impair its productivity for plants, but not

containing an excess of exchangeable sodium.

Sand. Individual rock or mineral fragments in soils, having diameters ranging from 0.5 to 2.0 millimeters. Usually sand grains consist chiefly of quartz but they may be of any mineral composition.

Scorch. A condition brought about by bacteria, drought, heat, excess salts, wind, fungi or sun exposure; characterized by the yellowing or browning of a plant's foliage.

Seed. The small grains produced by flowering plants containing embryos that germinate to produce new plants.

Seedbed. The name given to a garden soil prepared to receive seeds or plants. Prepared by plowing and disking, tilling or spading and raking.

Seed flats. Boxes used for starting seeds, generally 3 to 4 inches deep; a popular size is 14 inches wide, 24 inches long.

Seed germination. The beginning of growth of the young plant in a seed when heat, moisture and air are provided.

Seedling. The young plant emerging from a germinating seed. If seeds are sown thickly in a seedbed, for example, they soon begin to fight for sufficient growing room. As their true leaves appear, they should be transplanted to bed or box until they are ready for transplanting to the garden.

Seedling

Seed starters. Known commercially as peat pots, e.g., Jiffy 7's, Kys Kubes, Fertl Cubes. Small growing units containing nutrients for seed germination. Can be transplanted directly into soil.

Seed tapes. Seeds pre-spaced and enclosed into a water-soluble plasticlike tape. When tape is planted, covered with soil and watered, it dissolves, and the seeds germinate.

Sheath. A separate part of a plant, tubular in structure, that encases the lower end of a stalk.

Sheath

Short-season crop. A crop that grows and produces its harvest within one or two months.

Shredder, shredder-bagger, shredder-grinder, chipper. Machines designed to shred garden debris, branches, leaves,

sod and so forth. Many also mix soil and concrete and pulverize rock for decorative mulches.

Shrub. Generally smaller than a tree, a woody perennial that usually has numerous stems growing from its roots.

Side-dressing. Fertilizers applied close enough to a plant so that its root zone is provided with food.

Side-Dressing

Silt. A fine-grained type of soil sediment resulting from deposits of streams. When properly mixed with organic matter, it makes an excellent garden soil. Fine particles, 0.02 to 0.002 mm. in diameter.

Slip. A cutting pulled, broken or cut from a woody or herbaceous plant.

Small fruits. As distinguished from tree fruits, these are fruits produced from vines or low-growing plants.

Sod. A surface of earth covered with grass. Also, a section of ground containing top growth of grass and the matted roots used to cover bare soil.

Sodding. The process of covering a given area with turf grass. Sods of turf grass with adhering soil can be used in sizes varying from small plugs or strips to large blocks or squares.

Sodic soil. A soil which contains an excess of sodium, usually with a pH greater than 8.5, and is also non-saline.

Soil. (1) The dynamic natural bodies of the surface of the earth in which land plants grow. (2) Composed of a mineral fraction and an organic fraction, with living forms. (3) Results from the integrated effect of climate and living matter acting upon parent material, as conditioned by weather over periods of time.

Soil aeration. As a process, the loosening or puncturing of soil by mechanical means in order to increase water and air permeability.

Soil amendment. Addition to the soil of natural or synthesized chemical or mineral materials designed to improve the soil's drainage or moisture retention or aeration.

Soil-borne fungi. Small, non-green plants that live in the soil, some of which are capable of causing plant disease.

Soil crusting. The formation of a hard layer of soil on the soil surface.

Soil improvement. Making soils more productive by such practices as adding organic matter, fertilizers and lime.

Soilless culture. The practice of growing plants in a nutrient solution without the use of soil. (See Hydroponics.)

Soil sterilization. Accomplished by fumigation—chemical, heat or steam; a process by which soil is made free of harmful organisms.

Soil testing. A scientific analysis of a soil sample's acidity, texture and chemical composition in order to gauge the suitability of the soil for certain uses or to determine the modifications necessary to adapt it to a desired use.

Soil texture. The size of the soil particles giving the proportion of clay, sand and silt in a given soil.

Species. A group of plants closely resembling each other and which interbreed freely.

Sphagnum moss. A group of mosses that grow in bogs. Peat moss is often formed in whole or part from sphagnum in decomposed form, but they have different effects on the soil. Also available packaged in whole pieces, dried or fresh; useful to line wire baskets and the like as planters.

Sphagnum peat. Containing a minimum of 66⅔% sphagnum fibers by weight (a peat that has been oven-dried).

Spike. An elongated flower cluster having blossoms sessile (attached directly by the base) or on stalks that are unusually short.

Spreader. A mechanism used for seeding and fertilizing. Or a plant that grows wider than tall. Also refers to certain materials added to sprays to aid in distribution.

Spreading. The procedure used to apply grass seed or fertilizer to soil or lawns by use of a spreading device.

Sprig. A small twig or shoot.

Sprout. The term used to denote the development of new growth from seed. Also the development of new shoots.

Standard. A shrub, herb or tree that has a single upright treelike stem. Also refers to the upper, usually upright petal of an irregular flower, e.g. iris.

Standard

Starter solution. A chemical fertilizer first dissolved in water, then applied in the planting hole or around the roots of seedlings that have been newly transplanted. Helps them to withstand the shock of being moved; it also speeds up the seedlings' development.

Sterile. Soil that is free of living organisms. Also, the condition of plants that are unable to reproduce, either because their seeds cannot germinate or because they do not bear any fruit.

Sterilize. Ridding the soil, by steam or chemical means, of fungi, bacteria, worms and other living organisms that are harmful to plants.

Stolon. A horizontal branch from the base of a plant that produces new plants from buds at its tip. It creeps along the surface of the ground, rooting now and then and forming new plants (e.g., Bermuda grass).

Strain. A group of similar plants of the same variety with a common characteristic of improved growth or quality, e.g., size, color, vigor, disease-resistance.

Stress. The external factors that inhibit perfect plant growth, i.e. all factors pertaining to the wide-ranging conditions of nature.

Subirrigation. The practice of watering from underneath. Such irrigation ranges from elaborate watering systems through conduit beneath the ground, to simply placing a newly potted plant in a tray of water to absorb moisture by capillary action. See also Drip irrigation.

Subsoil. The layers of soil lying beneath the 6-8 inches of topsoil. Often more compacted, less fertile, and containing less organic matter.

Succession. The normal sequence of crops, from cool-weather kinds (e.g., lettuce, peas) to warm-weather varieties (e.g., corn, beans) to cool fall varieties like cauliflower or cabbage. Succession can mean a wide variety of vegetables for one's dinner menu if the gardener plants small amounts of the same vegetable at frequent intervals.

Succulent. A plant having thickened, juicy stems or leaves (or both) that act as depositories of moisture against a time of drought. Its native habitats are hot, dry desert regions. A succulent makes a fine houseplant requiring little care.

Sucker. A shoot that springs up from underground, grows from trunk or branch or the lower part of a plant—an unwanted shoot.

Sucker

Synthesis. Combination of simple molecules to form another substance—e.g., the union of carbon dioxide and water under the action of sunlight in photosynthesis to form carbohydrates.

Systemic. A pesticide that is absorbed into the system of a plant, causing the plant juice to become toxic to its enemies.

Tamping. The practice of firming loosened soil into which seeds or new transplants have been placed.

Taproot. A main root descending downward in the soil and giving off small lateral roots. Examples: carrots, dandelions.

Taproot

Tender plant. A plant that is injured or killed by even a light frost, or too much heat.

Tendril. Leafless threadlike organs on many vines that help the vine both to climb and cling to its support.

Tendril

Tensiometer. A device for measuring the tension with which water is held in the soil, helpful in determining when to irrigate.

Timed-release fertilizers. See Controlled-release fertilizers.

Topsoil. A general term used in at least 4 different senses: (1) A presumed fertile soil or soil material, usually rich in organic matter, used to topdress road banks, lawns and gardens; (2) the surface plowable layer of a soil, and thus a synonym for surface soil; (3) the original or present dark-colored upper soil, which ranges from a mere fraction of an inch to 2 or 3 feet on different kinds of soil; and (4) the original or present "A" horizon, varying widely among different kinds of soil.

Toxic material. Poisonous materials used to kill pests or those materials that may be poisonous to the growing plant.

Trace elements. Minute quantities of mineral nutrients that are as vital to plant life as are the major nutrients. Examples of trace elements are copper, iron, manganese and zinc.

Transpiration. The process by which moisture is emitted from plant leaves through transmission of water absorbed through its roots. Dictated by humidity, wind, temperature and available water.

Transplant. A plant produced from seed germinated in a favorable environment for later planting in an area where the plant is to grow to maturity. As seedlings begin to crowd, they should be transplanted to a second flat or container and allowed enough space to grow until they are ready to be set out in the garden.

Turf. A dense or matted growth of grasses with intermingled roots that form a mat.

Turgid. A term used to describe plant cells having adequate moisture to cause the cells to expand fully.

Variety. A subgroup of plants in a species (the lowest or final natural classification) with particular like characteristics. Each variety within a species keeps the basic character of the species, but has at least one, sometimes more, individual characteristics of its own.

Vermiculite. A mica product expanded by heat treatment to form an extremely lightweight material. It is used either for soil conditioning or as a rooting medium for plants. It is a product often used in a synthetic soil formula.

Viable seed. A seed containing a small living plant (embryo) that will begin to grow once conditions necessary for germination (sprouting) are provided.

Virgin soil. A soil that has not been significantly disturbed from its natural environment.

Water requirement. Generally, the amount of water required by plants for satisfactory growth during the season. The water requirement varies with climatic conditions, soil moisture and other soil characteristics.

Water table. The upper limit of the part of the soil or underlying rock material that is wholly saturated with water. In some places an upper, or perched, water table may be separated from a lower one by a dry zone.

Waterlogged. A condition of soil in which both large and small pore spaces are filled with water.

Weathering. The physical and chemical disintegration and decomposition of rocks and minerals.

Weed. A plant growing out of place.

Index

Tables of weights and measures

Linear measure

12 inches (in.)	= 1 foot (ft.)
3 feet	= 1 yard (yd.)
5½ yards	= 1 rod (rd.), pole, or perch (16½ ft.)
40 rods	= 1 furlong (fur.) = 220 yards = 660 feet
8 furlongs	= 1 statute mile (mi.) = 1,760 yards = 5,280 feet
3 land miles	= 1 league
5,280 feet	= 1 statute or land mile
6,076 feet	= 1 international nautical mile

Area measure

Squares and cubes of units are sometimes abbreviated by using "superior" figures. For example, ft² means square foot, and ft³ means cubic foot.

144 square inches	= 1 square foot
9 square feet	= 1 square yard = 1,296 square inches
30¼ square yards	= 1 square rod = 272¼ square feet
160 square rods	= 1 acre = 4,840 square yards = 43,560 square feet
640 acres	= 1 square mile
1 mile square	= 1 section (of land)
6 miles square	= 1 township = 36 sections = 36 square miles

Cubic measure

1,728 cubic inches	= 1 cubic foot
27 cubic feet	= 1 cubic yard

Liquid measure

Teaspoons
3 tsp. = 1 Tbs.

Tablespoons

2 Tbs.	= ⅛ cup or 1 fl. oz.
4 Tbs.	= ¼ cup or 2 fl. oz.
8 Tbs.	= ½ cup or ¼ pint
16 Tbs.	= 1 cup or ½ pint

Cups, Pints, Quarts

2 cupfuls	= 1 pint or 16 fl. ozs.
2 pints	= 1 quart
4 quarts	= 1 gallon

Dry measure

When necessary to distinguish the dry pint or quart from the liquid pint or quart, the word "dry" should be used in combination with the name or abbreviation of the dry unit.

2 pints	= 1 quart (= 67.2 cubic inches)
8 quarts	= 1 peck (pk.) (= 637.6 cubic inches) = 16 pints
4 pecks	= 1 bushel (bu.) (= 2550.42 cubic inches) = 32 quarts

Metric system

The United States is the only major industrial power that has not adopted the International System of Measurement Units (Système International — SI) exclusively. Popularly known as the Metric System — from the Greek word *metron*, a measure — it was created by the French Scientific Academy in 1790. It is considered the most efficient and logical measurement system ever devised. There is now a trend in this country to adopt SI on a nationwide basis.

UNITS OF WEIGHT

Pound - ounce	Metric
220.46 LBS.	100 KG.
100 LBS.	45,359 KG.
2.2046 LBS.	1 KILOGRAM
1.1023 LBS.	500 GR.
1 LB. or 16 OZ.	453.59 GR.
½ POUND or 8 OZ.	226.78 GR.
4 OZ.	113.39 GR.
3.5274 OZ.	100 GRAMS
1 OZ.	28.35 GRAMS
1/16 OUNCE	1.771 GRAMS

UNITS OF LENGTH

Feet - inches	Metric
1 MILE or 5,280 FT.	1.6093 KM.
0.621 MILE	1000 METER or 1 KM.
328 FT.	100 METER
3.281 FT.	100 CM. or 1 METER
1 YARD or 3 FT. or 36 IN.	91.44 CM.
1 FOOT or 12 IN.	30.48 CM.
1 INCH	2.540 CM.
0.3937 INCH	1 CENTIMETER

UNITS OF AREA

Acres	Metric
1 SQ. MILE or 640 AC.	259 HECTARES or 2.59 SQ. KM.
.3861 SQ. MI. or 247 AC.	100 HA. or 1 SQ. KM.
24.71 ACRES	10 HA.
10 ACRES	4.047 HA.
2.471 ACRES	1 HA.
1 ACRE	.4047 HA.

LIQUID MEASURE

Gallon - ounces	Metric
2.642 GAL.	10 LITER
1 GALLON	3.7852 LITER
1.0567 QUARTS	1 LITER
1 QUART or 32 FL. OZ.	0.9463 LITER
1 PINT or 16 FL. OZ.	0.4732 LITER
1 CUP or 8 FLUID OZ.	0.2366 LITER
1 FLUID OUNCE	0.0295 LITER

So you're about to water.

To cover 1000 sq. ft. with an inch of water takes 624 gallons.

One gallon/min (gpm) = 1440 gallons/day

10.4 gallons/min applies one inch of water over 1000 sq. ft. every hour.

Gallons/minutes × 8.03 = cubic ft./hour.

One gallon of water weighs 8.34 pounds.